Discover ENGLISH 1

Workbook

with CD-ROM

T0352588

KATE WAKEMAN

Hello

My Picture Dictionary

Objects

1 Read page 4 of the Student's Book again. What are their favourite things?

Gemma	Felix	Monica

dog		

2 Complete the table for you.

Name	Age	Class	Favourite colour	Favourite thing

my words

Do you know more words for objects and colours?
Write them here.

_____

_____

_____

_____

_____

3 Write the words in the correct column.

~~black~~ skateboard eleven purple Gemma Monica
yellow Felix Year 6 red ten dog MP3 player

Age	Class	Colour	Name	Thing
		black		

to be

4 ☆ Read the texts. True or false?

Hi! I'm Flavia. I'm in Year 5. I'm ten. My favourite colour is yellow. My favourite thing is my dog. He isn't black. He's white.

Hello! My name's Marcin. I'm eleven. I'm in Year 6. My favourite colour is red. My dog is my favourite thing. He's black.

Marcin

1	I'm in Year 6.	_true_
2	My favourite colour isn't red.	_____
3	My favourite colour is black.	_____
4	My dog isn't white.	_____
5	My dog is black.	_____

Flavia

6	I'm ten.	_____
7	I'm in Year 6.	_____
8	My dog is white.	_____
9	My favourite colour isn't red.	_____

5 ☆ Write the words in full.

I'm	¹ **I am**	I'm not	⁸ _____
You're	² _____	You aren't	⁹ **you are not**
He's	³ _____	He isn't	¹⁰ _____
She's	⁴ _____	She isn't	¹¹ _____
It's	⁵ _____	It isn't	¹² _____
We're	⁶ _____	We aren't	¹³ _____
They're	⁷ _____	They aren't	¹⁴ _____

6 ☆ Complete the sentences. Use *'m*, *'re*, *is*, or *are*.

1 I **'m** ten.
2 You _____ eleven.
3 We _____ in Year 6.
4 Felix _____ in Year 5.
5 My favourite colours _____ black and yellow.
6 My favourite thing _____ my skateboard.

to be: questions

7 ☆ Match the words.

1 Are you   a are you?
2 Is your favourite thing   b your name?
3 What's   c ten?
4 How old   d blue?
5 Is your favourite colour   e your MP3 player?

8 ☆☆ Complete the sentences. Use *Is*, *Am*, or *Are*.

1 **Is** he ten?
2 _____ they in Year 5?
3 _____ she in Year 6?
4 _____ you eleven?
5 _____ I eleven?
6 _____ it a dog?

A New Home

Favourite things

1 Read the text. Complete the chart.

Hello! I'm Emma. My family are from Detroit. Detroit is in the USA. Our new home is in New York. My favourite baseball team is the New York Yankees. My favourite things are my *baseball* cap and shirt. They're great!

Emma	from: _Detroit, USA_
New home	in: _____
Favourite team	_____
Favourite things	1 _____
	2 _____

2 Find these words in the word square.

~~FOOTBALL~~   BASEBALL CAP   CD PLAYER
MOBILE PHONE   SHIRT   FAMILY   WATCH

M	E	R	A	D	O	G	A	D	S	B
O	R	W	E	R	O	R	S	F	W	A
B	T	A	H	G	G	S	C	C	D	S
I	H	T	G	U	T	H	V	D	T	E
L	U	C	D	A	S	I	G	P	Y	B
E	O	H	F	X	W	R	K	L	J	A
P	P	D	F	O	O	T	B	A	L	L
H	L	W	J	F	V	J	K	Y	U	L
O	M	K	I	T	H	P	O	E	S	C
N	V	L	P	H	U	L	P	R	G	A
E	F	E	F	A	M	I	L	Y	H	P

Plurals

3 Write the plural endings.

Singular	Plural
1 shirt	shirt _s_
2 match	match _____
3 thing	thing _____
4 camera	camera _____
5 city	cit _____
6 watch	watch _____
7 family	famil _____
8 team	team _____

4 Circle the correct words.

Hi! I'm Felix. My ¹(home)/ homes is in England. My favourite football ² **team / teams** is Chelsea.
Their ³ **match / matches** are great. Their football ⁴ **shirt / shirts** are blue.

My favourite ⁵ **thing / things** are my skateboard and my Chelsea ⁶ **watch / watches**.

Possessive adjectives

5 ☆ Complete the table.

I	*my*
[1] _____	your
he	[4] _____
she	[5] _____
[2] _____	its
we	[6] _____
[3] _____	their

6 ☆☆ Write sentences.

1 My name's James.   *His name's James.*

2 My name's Anne.   *Her* _____

3 It's my CD player.   _____

4 It's our dog.   _____

5 It's my camera.   _____

6 They're our baseball caps! _____

Countries

7 Write the words.

		Country	Nationality
1	En …	*England*	*English*
2	Pol …	*Poland*	
3	Braz …		
4	Arg …		
5	Russ …		
6	Gre …		
7	Port …		

8 Complete the sentences. Use these words.

Poland	Polish	England	English
Brazil	Brazilian	Turkey	Turkish
Italy	Italian	Greece	Greek
~~Russia~~	Russian	Portugal	Portuguese

1 I'm from R *ussia* .
2 Ewa is Pol _____ .
3 I'm from T _____ .
4 Querida is from Por _____ .
5 Maria is B _____ .
6 Are you E _____ ?
7 Lucia is I _____ .
8 Theo is from G _____ .

9 Circle the correct word.

My favourite star is Nani (Luis Carlos Almeida da Cunha). He's from [1] **Portuguese** / **(Portugal)** but [2] **his** / **her** home is in [3] **England** / **English**. [4] **His** / **Her** football team is Manchester United and [5] **their** / **our** football shirts are red.

Earth Explorer

this, that, these, those

1 ⭐ Label the pictures. Use *this*, *that*, *these* or *those*.

1 _these_

2 _____

3 _____

4 _____

2 ⭐ Write the plurals.

1 this baseball cap _these baseball caps_
2 that team _____
3 this colour _____
4 this CD player _____
5 that watch _____
6 this city _____

3 ⭐⭐ Make these sentences plural.

1 This is my friend.
These are my friends.
2 That is our camera.
_____
3 This is my favourite colour.
_____
4 This is my favourite star.
_____
5 That is my shirt.
_____
6 That is my dog.
_____

4 Put the stickers in the correct places.

┌─────────────────────┐
│   │
│   Sticker   │
│   │
└─────────────────────┘

① These are my favourite things: my watch, my skateboard and my football shirt. The skateboard is yellow and red and the shirt is red too! My watch is black. They're great things!

┌─────────────────────┐
│   │
│   Sticker   │
│   │
└─────────────────────┘

② My three favourite things? They're here. This watch is pink and it's great. My mobile phone is purple and this football shirt is red and yellow.

Fiz's Learning Blog

Learning things in pairs

These are some pairs from this unit. Make cards. Test yourself!

singular / plural

this | these   city | cities

countries / nationalities

England | English

subject pronouns / possessive adjectives

I | my

1 People

My Picture Dictionary

Appearance

1 Label the pictures.

f _a_ _t_

_ _ a l _ _ / _ _ _ _ _ _ t

_ _ _ _ d - l _ _ _ _ _ _ _ _

_ _ h _ _ _ _

o _ _ _ / _ o _ _ _ g

_ _ _ l _

2 Complete the puzzle.

good-looking   fat   short   thin   young   old   ugly   tall

my words

Do you know any more
appearance words?
Write them here.

_____

_____

_____

_____

_____

_____

Talking Tips!

1 Find two Talking Tips in the snail. Match them with the pictures (a and b).

PHOTO HE'S FUNNY FRIEND COOL! FRISBEE HELLO

1 _____
2 _____

3 Read the sentences. True or false?

1 The photos are Ben's. _**true**_
2 A dog is in the photo. _____
3 Bingo isn't the dog. _____
4 The mobile phone isn't a camera. _____

2 Complete the dialogue. Use the Talking Tips from Exercise 1.

Felix Is this your camera, Ben?
Ben Yes, it is. It's my mobile phone too.
Felix It's great!
Ben Look at my photos.
Felix Ha! Ha! ¹_____ ! Is he your dog?
Ben Yes, he is. He's my dog, Bingo. He's got my Frisbee in his mouth!
Felix That's a great photo. And this photo?
Ben That's me and Bingo in Central Park – in New York!
Felix ²_____ !

The beach

4 What's in the beach bag?

1 _a drink_
2 _____
3 _____
4 _____
5 _____

have got / haven't got

5 ☆ Write the words in full.

I've got	¹ *I have got*	I haven't got	⁷ *she has not got*
you've got	2 _____	you haven't got	8 _____
he's got	3 _____	he hasn't got	9 _____
she's got	4 _____	she hasn't got	10 _____
we've got	5 _____	we haven't got	11 _____
they've got	6 _____	they haven't got	12 _____

6 ☆ Write the sentences with short forms.

1 I have got a drink.
   I've got a drink
2 She has got a camera.
   _____
3 He has got a dog.
   _____
4 We have got ice creams.
   _____
5 They have got a family photo.
   _____
6 We have got a beach bag.
   _____

7 ☆☆ Complete the sentences. Use *has got*, *have got*, *hasn't got* or *haven't got*.

1 Ben **has got** got an ice cream. ✓
2 Felix _____ a mobile phone. ✗
3 Gemma _____ a dog. ✓
4 Felix and Monica _____ cameras. ✗
5 Felix and Gemma _____ drinks. ✓
6 Monica _____ a dog. ✗
7 Ben _____ a mobile phone. ✓

8 ☆☆☆ Complete the sentences.

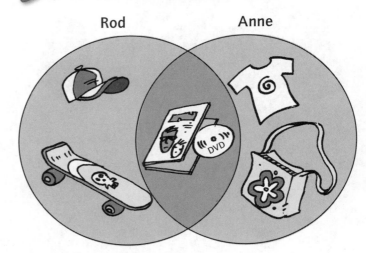

Rod   Anne

1 Rod **has got** a baseball cap.
2 He _____ a beach bag.
3 Anne _____ a _____ .
4 She _____ a _____ too.
5 Rod and Anne _____ a _____ .

9 Circle the words.

Family

1 Label the people in Ben's family. Use these words.

> sister (x 2)   cousin   uncle   granddad
> granny   mum   ~~dad~~

2 _____

3 _____

1 *dad*

6 _____

5 _____   7 _____

4 _____

2 Complete the sentences about Ben's cousin, Danny. Use family words from Exercise 1.

1 Danny's **_dad_** is Frank. Frank is my **_uncle_** .
2 Danny's mum is Sarah. Sarah is my
   _____ .
3 My _____ is my dad's mum.
4 She is Frank's _____ too.
5 My _____ is Frank's dad too.
6 My sisters are Danny's _____ .

3 Read about Amy. True or false?

> Hi! I'm Amy. I'm from Liverpool. It's in England. I've got a brother but I haven't got a sister. My mum and dad are from Manchester. I've got two dogs. Their names are Ronnie and Reggie. The dogs are brothers! I've got a cat too. His name is Smokey. He's black and white. Have you got a cat? Have you got a dog?

1 Amy is from Liverpool.   *true*
2 Liverpool is an English city.   _____
3 Amy has got a brother and a sister.   _____
4 Her mum and dad are from London.   _____
5 Her cat is black and white.   _____
6 Amy has got three dogs.   _____

Have you got …?

4 ☆ Complete the questions. Use *have* or *has*.

1 **_Have_** I got a sister?
2 _____ you got a brother?
3 _____ she got an uncle?
4 _____ we got cousins?
5 _____ he got a brother?
6 _____ they got sisters?

5 ⭐⭐ **Complete the questions.**

1 (Sue and Trisha) **_Have they got_** sisters?
2 (You and me) _____ cousins?
3 (Maria) _____ a granddad?
4 (Peter) _____ a sister?
5 (Me) _____ an aunt?
6 (Mike and Pippa) _____ brothers?

6 ⭐ **Answer the questions about you.**
Answer _Yes, I have_, or _No, I haven't_.

1 Have you got sisters? _____
2 Have you got brothers? _____
3 Have you got a granddad? _____
4 Have you got a granny? _____

7 ⭐⭐ **Write questions about Ben's family.**
Answer the questions.

1 got sisters?
Has he got sisters?
Yes, he has.

2 got a brother?
_____ ?
_____

3 got a granddad?
_____ ?
_____

4 got an aunt?
_____ ?
_____

5 got an uncle?
_____ ?
_____

8 ⭐⭐ **Read about Cristina's family. Write questions and answers. Use _have got_ or _has got_.**

My Family

Hi! I'm Cristina. My family is from Argentina but our home is in the USA.

I've got two brothers and a sister. My mum and dad are here in the USA, but my granny and granddad are in Argentina. It's great in Argentina! They've got two horses and three dogs. We've got two cats.

My favourite thing is my new mobile phone. It's got a camera and an MP3 player! Wow!

1 she / brothers?
Has he got brothers?
Yes, he has.

2 she / a sister?
_____?
_____

3 granny and granddad / horses?
_____?
_____

4 granny and granddad / cats?
_____?
_____

5 she / horses?
_____?
_____

6 she / a mobile phone?
_____?
_____

7 she / a camera?
_____?
_____

Possessive 's

1 ☆ Follow the lines. Complete the sentences.

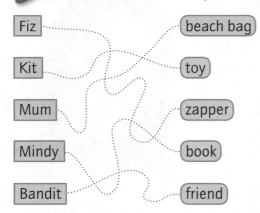

Fiz · Kit · Mum · Mindy · Bandit

beach bag · toy · zapper · book · friend

1 That's *Fiz's* zapper.
2 It's _____ beach bag.
3 This is _____ toy.
4 This is _____ friend.
5 That's _____ book.

2 ☆ Look at the table. Complete the sentences.

Monica	Ben	Felix	Gemma
mobile phone	camera	toy	book
beach bag	MP3 player	CD player	watch
baseball cap	frisbee	drink	towel

1 It's *Monica's* mobile phone.
2 It's _____ toy.
3 It's _____ watch.
4 It's _____ MP3 player.
5 It's _____ baseball cap.
6 It's _____ drink.

3 ☆☆ Write more sentences about the other things in the table.

It's Ben's camera.

_____
_____
_____
_____
_____

Describing people

4 Choose words and describe your friend.

My friend's name is _____ . He / She is **tall / short**. He / She has got **blue / brown / black / green** eyes and **short / long** hair. **His / her** hair is **blonde / brown / black / red**.

5 Describe you.

My name is _____
I am _____ .
I've got _____ eyes and _____ hair.
My hair is _____ .

6 Describe Fiz and Bandit.

Fiz has got *green hair* and _____
_____ .
He's _____ and
_____ .
Bandit has got _____
and _____ .
He's _____ and
_____ .

7 Read the description and find the correct sticker.

> Sticker

Hello! My name is Yooha and I'm from planet Poogle. My body is very long and it's orange. I've got short black hair on my body. I'm very good-looking!

8 Put the other sticker here. Complete the description. Use these words.

> long   white   eyes   ~~tall~~

> Sticker

Hi! I'm Wizzo from planet Wiz. I'm not ¹*__tall__* and I've got ² _____ blue hair. My eyes are ³ _____ . I've got extra ⁴ _____ in my hair — they're great!

9 Complete the report. Use these words.

> is   Have   Kit's   ~~got~~

REPORT FROM OUTER SPACE

Hello Fiz!

We've ¹*__got__* your report. ² _____ you got your zapper? What ³ _____ Bandit? Is ⁴ _____ mum a friend?

Bye!

Your friends from outer space.

Fiz's Learning Blog

Remember words

To remember appearance words, draw picture words.

To remember family words, label a family photo.

mum   dad

brother   me   sister

Cool People!

Reading

1 Read the text. True or false?

My favourite star is Justin Timberlake. He's American. He's very good-looking. He's got blonde hair and blue eyes and he's tall (1.85m). He's got two brothers but he hasn't got a sister. His favourite things are his cars and ice cream! His favourite colour is blue and his favourite team is the North Carolina Tar Heels.

1	He's from the USA.	*true*
2	His eyes are brown.	_____
3	He isn't short.	_____
4	He's got two sisters.	_____
5	Ice cream is a favourite thing.	_____
6	Brown is his favourite colour.	_____
7	He hasn't got a favourite team.	_____

2 Match the photos and the descriptions.

 **a** Sulley

b Cruella DeVil

 **c** Wallace

 **d** Scooby Doo

1 She's in an American film. She's got white and black hair and she's ugly. **_b_**

2 He's an American film star! He's big and he's got blue hair. He's got black eyes. He's good-looking …! _____

3 He's in American films. He's got brown hair and brown eyes. He's good looking … and he's a dog! _____

4 He's an English film star. He's got black eyes and he hasn't got any hair. He's got a big mouth and he's got a dog too! _____

Writing

3 This is a description of Monica's favourite star. It's all mixed up! Write it again in the correct order.

Hi! My ⬚very good-looking.⬚ is Brad Pitt. He's tall and ⬚the USA.⬚ He's from ⬚favourite star⬚ He has got ⬚film⬚ and he's ⬚got blonde hair.⬚ He's a ⬚blue eyes⬚ star.

Hi! My favourite star is Brad Pitt. _____

_____

_____

_____

_____

_____

②Homes

My Picture Dictionary

Rooms

1 Write the words.

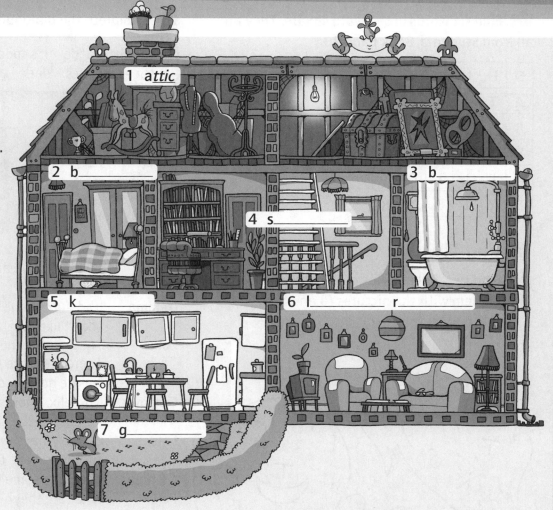

1 *attic*

2 b_____

3 b_____

4 s_____

5 k_____

6 l_____ r_____

7 g_____

2 Answer questions about your home.
Write *Yes, it has*. Or *No, it hasn't*.

1 Has it got stairs?
_____

2 Has it got an attic?
_____

3 Has it got a kitchen?
_____

4 Has it got a garden?
_____

my words

Do you know more words for homes?
Write them here.

_____
_____
_____
_____
_____
_____

Discover **5** extra words. Go to page 87.

1 Find six words in the word square. They are all from Students' Book page 20.

D	H	U	A	R	G
A	T	T	I	C	H
R	N	A	R	A	O
K	E	B	L	T	S
H	E	L	L	O	T
S	Y	E	O	T	R

Talking Tips!

2 Find two Talking Tips in the ghosts. Match them with the pictures (a and b).

1 _____

2 _____

3 Complete the dialogue. Use these words

It's a joke   attic   It's spooky!
frisbee   comics   ~~dark~~

Felix Gemma, come and see! There's an old box.

Gemma It's ¹ **dark** in the attic. I don't like it. ² _____

Felix These are Granddad's things. There are some books here – look! Has he got any comics?

Gemma No, Felix. There aren't any ³ _____

Felix Oh. … What's this? There's an old cupboard here. Look.

Gemma There are some toys here.

Felix What are they?

Gemma There's a ⁴ _____ and there are some old footballs.

Felix Let's play frisbee!

Gemma Felix, no! Not in the ⁵ _____ !

CRASH!

Granddad Felix? Gemma?

Felix Look Granddad! There's a ghost!

Granddad What? Where?

Gemma ⁶ _____ , Granddad! Felix!!

Furniture

4 Write the words.

1 _sofa_

2 _____

3 _____

4 _____

5 _____

6 _____

7 _____

8 _____

5 Complete the crossword. Find the secret word!

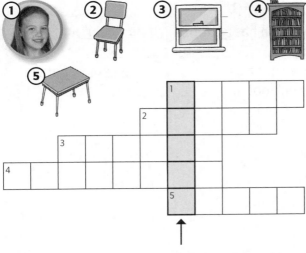

The secret word is

_____

there is / there are

6 ☆ Circle the correct word.

GRANDDAD'S ATTIC

1 (There's) / There are a mirror in the attic.
2 There isn't / There aren't any ghosts.
3 There's / There are some old chairs.
4 There's / There are an old table.
5 There's / There are a bookcase.
6 There isn't / There aren't any windows.
7 There's / There are a message in the mirror.

7 ☆ Complete the sentences. Use 's, are, or aren't.

In Granddad's attic there ¹ **are** some old chairs.
There ² _____ an old table and a bookcase.
It's dark – there ³ _____ any windows.
There ⁴ _____ a message in the mirror but
there ⁵ _____ any ghosts.

8 ☆☆ Complete the sentences. Use some, any or a.

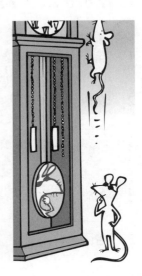

Hi! I'm Mike the Mouse.
My home is tall and thin.
There are ¹ **some** windows
but there isn't
² _____ door.
There's ³ _____
bed and there are
⁴ _____ funny
mirrors too, but there aren't
⁵ _____ sofas or
chairs.

9 ☆☆☆ Write sentences about your living room at home.

There's a _____
in my living room. _____
are _____ _____
too. _____ aren't
_____
_____ .

2ᵇ Fun Homes

Prepositions of place

1 ☆ Complete the poem. Use these words.

~~under~~   on   in   next to   behind

There's a cat ¹ **_under_** the table.
The cat's name is Mabel.
There's a cat ² _____ the chair.
It's Mabel's friend Claire.
There's a cat ³ _____ the bed.
His name is Fred.
There's a cat ⁴ _____ the TV.
And her name is Evie.
There's a cat ⁵ _____ the cupboard.
He hasn't got a name.

Is there … / are there …

2 ☆☆ Order the words.

1   there   chairs   Are   any   in the bedroom
    Are there any chairs in the bedroom?

2   computer   there   in the room   Is   a
    _____?

3   any   in the kitchen   cupboards   Are   there
    _____?

4   Are   windows   any   there   in the classroom
    _____?

5   there   a   Is   in your bedroom   desk
    _____?

6   a   Is   there   on the boat   bed
    _____?

7   trees   in your garden   there   Are   any
    _____?

3 Complete Ben's description of his home.

My home has got three ¹ b **_e_** **_d_** **_r_** **_o_** **_o_** **_m_** **_s_**
and two ² __ __ __ h __ r __ __ __ __ .
We've got a small ³ __ __ a __ __ e __ , but we
haven't got an ⁴ __ t t __ __ .

4 ⭐ **Read Monica's webpage about Jack's fun home. Complete the questions and answers.**

Jack's Fun Home

Here's Jack's fun home – it's a train!
It's very long, but it isn't very big inside.
In the train there's a long table and a
small kitchen. In the kitchen there's a
small fridge. The kitchen is next to the
living room. He's got a TV and a sofa
in the train. There are some bedrooms
in the train and there are lots of big
windows so it isn't dark. Outside he's
got a very big garden. It's a great home
– it's good fun!

1   _Is_ there a table?
    Yes, _____ is.
2   Is _____ a TV?
    _____ there is.
3   _____ there any beds?
    Yes, there _____
4   Are _____ any stairs?
    No, there _____
5   _____ there a big fridge?
    _____ , there isn't.
6   Is _____ an attic?
    No, there _____

5 ⭐⭐ **Write more questions and answers about Jack's home.**

1   kitchen (✓)
    Is there a kitchen? Yes there is.
2   fridge (✓)
    _____
3   bookcase (✗)
    _____
4   bedrooms (✓)
    _____
5   cupboards (✗)
    _____
6   windows (✓)
    _____
7   garden (✓)
    _____
8   ghost (✗)
    _____

6 ⭐ **Answer these questions about your house.**

1   Is there a TV in the living room?
    _____
2   Is there a TV in your bedroom?
    _____
3   Is your bedroom big or small?
    _____
4   Are there any cupboards in your bedroom?
    _____
5   Is the kitchen big or small?
    _____
6   Is the house old or new?
    _____

7 ⭐⭐ **Write sentences about your house. Choose furniture and objects.**

There's a _____
in the kitchen. There are _____
_____ too.
_____ in the living room.
_____ in my bedroom.
I've got _____ too.

1 Read about Warwick Castle. True or false?

This is Warwick Castle. It's in England. It's very big and there are lots of rooms in Warwick Castle. There are very big gardens too. There are lots of trees and flowers. Are there any ghosts? Yes, there are! Come and see them!

1 Warwick Castle is in the USA. _false_
2 It's a small castle. _____
3 There are lots of rooms in the castle. _____
4 The gardens are small. _____
5 There aren't any trees. _____
6 There are some ghosts at Warwick Castle. _____

Giving instructions

2 Match the words.

1 Hurry   a there
2 Stay   b down
3 Be   c touch
4 Sit   d nice
5 Don't   e up

3 Find the imperatives.

1 e b t e q u i _Be_ _____
2 o n'd t a l k t _____ _____
3 y s t a e r t h e _____ _____
4 r r h u y p u _____ _____

4 Write the imperatives in the correct column.

Open   Listen   Don't talk
Don't sit down   Stay there   Be good

Positive	Negative
Open	

5 Complete the instructions.

1
L _ook_ at your book!

2
D _____
s _____ on the table!

3
O _____ the door!

4
St _____ up!

5
St _____
th _____!

6
B _____
q _____!

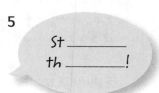

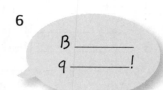

6 Look at the instructions in the box. Write three things the teacher tells you.

> ~~Hurry up!~~   Sit on the table!   Be quiet!
> Don't touch!   Be nice!   Sit down!   Be silly!
> Talk!   Stay there!   Wait!   Be good!

1 _Hurry up!_
2 _____
3 _____
4 _____

7 Write three more things your teacher tells you with *don't*.

1 _Don't sit on the table._
2 _____
3 _____
4 _____

8 Put the stickers in the correct place.

> ### Sticker
>
> ① I've got five brothers and sisters! There are four bedrooms in my house. My room has got two beds, for me and my brother. There is a long garden with lots of trees and we've got a big attic in the house — that's fun!

> ### Sticker
>
> ② In my home there are three bedrooms, one for mum and dad, one for my sister and one for me! We've got a big kitchen and lots of windows. There aren't any stairs and there isn't a garden. My home is a flat.

9 Complete the report. Use these words.

> listen   Stay   good   Who   ~~castle~~

REPORT FROM OUTER SPACE

We have got your report. Thank you. What is a ¹_castle_ ? ² _____ is Mindy? ³ _____ there on Earth and ⁴ _____ to Kit. Be ⁵ _____ !

Bye!

Your friends from outer space.

Fiz's Learning Blog

Remember words

Put English labels on furniture in your room!

chair

Vocabulary

1 Find the appearance adjectives.

1 l l a t _____   4 y g l u _____
2 r t h s o _____   5 u g o y n _____
3 n h i t _____

2 Complete the beach words.

1 t _ _ _ l   3 i _ _ cr _ _ _ _
2 f _ _ _ _ _ _   4 dr _ _ _

3 Match the words.

1 mum and   a sister
2 granny and   b dad
3 brother and   c aunt
4 uncle and   d granddad

___/13

Grammar

4 Complete. Use *have got*, *has got*, *haven't got*, or *hasn't got*.

1 Ben _____ his camera today. (✗)
2 Felix _____ his skateboard. (✓)
3 Gemma and Monica _____ a beach bag. (✓)
4 Ben and Felix _____ a frisbee. (✗)
5 _____ Gemma _____ a drink?
6 _____ Ben and Felix _____ a frisbee?

5 Complete the sentences.

1 Danny has got a dog.
   It's _____ dog.
2 Mum has got a cat.
   It's _____ cat.
3 Kit has got an MP3 player.
   It's _____ MP3 player.
4 Fiz has got a toy.
   It's _____ toy.

6 Circle the correct words.

1 There **isn't** / **aren't** a TV in our house.
2 There are **some** / **any** cupboards in the kitchen.
3 There are **a** / **some** big windows.
4 There **isn't** / **aren't** any toys in my room.

7 Complete the questions.

1 _____ any windows in the bathroom?
2 _____ any tables in the garden?
3 _____ a TV in the living room?
4 _____ a shower in the bathroom?

8 Write *behind*, *next to*, *under*, *in* or *on*.

1 It's _____ the box.
2 It's _____ the box.
3 It's _____ the box.
4 It's _____ the box.
5 It's _____ the box.

___/23

Functions

9 Complete the instructions.

1 _____ quiet.
2 _____ there.
3 _____ touch!
4 _____ up.

___/4

Your score	Your total score
	___/40

😄 30–40   🙂 20–30   ☹ 0–20

My Picture Dictionary

Animals

1 Label the animals.

> giraffe tiger squirrel monkey parrot
> chameleon turtle shark elephant bat dolphin

5 m _____

4 c _____

3 b _____

2 s _____

1 g *iraffe*

6 p _____

7 t _____

11 d _____

10 s _____

8 e _____

9 t _____

2 Match the word halves.

1	par	a	tle	
2	squi	b	phin	
3	mon	c	rrel	
4	tur	d	eleon	
5	dol	e	key	
6	cham	f	rot	

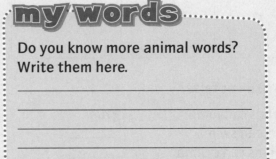

Do you know more animal words?
Write them here.

_____

_____

_____

_____

_____

_____

Action verbs

1 Complete the action verbs.

1 _jump_   2 s_____m   3 w_____ sk_____

4 c_____b   5 s_____g   6 f_____

7 p_____t

can / can't

2 ☆ Write the animals in the correct boxes.

> dolphins   tigers   monkeys   squirrels
> turtles   elephants   bats   sharks

Can jump	Can swim	Can climb	Can run
squirrels		_squirrels_	_squirrels_

3 ☆ True or false?

1 Squirrels can jump.   _true_
2 Tigers can swim.   _____
3 Dolphins can't climb.   _____
4 Giraffes can jump.   _____
5 Turtles can run.   _____
6 Bats can jump.   _____

4 ☆ Complete the sentences. Use _can_ or _can't_.

1 Tigers **_can_** jump.
2 Dolphins _____ swim.
3 Turtles _____ water ski.
4 Parrots _____ fly.
5 Monkeys _____ climb.
6 Elephants _____ jump.

5 Look at the table.

	Monica	Gemma	Felix
run	✓	✓	✓
climb	✗	✓	✓
swim	✓	✓	✗
sing	✗	✗	✓
dance	✓	✓	✓
play music	✓	✗	✗

a ☆ Who is it?

1 She can run. _Monica, Gemma_
2 She can swim. _____
3 She can't climb. _____
4 She can play music. _____
5 She can climb. _____
6 She can dance. _____

b ☆ Complete the sentences. Use _can_ or _can't_.

Monica
1 She **_can_** run.
2 She _____ climb.
3 She _____ sing.
4 She _____ swim.

Gemma
5 She _____ climb.
6 She _____ sing.
7 She _____ dance.
8 She _____ play music.

c ⭐⭐ Write four sentences about Felix.

1 *He can run.*
2 _____
  _____
3 _____
  _____
4 _____
  _____
5 _____
  _____

d ⭐⭐ Write about Gemma.

1 Two things she can do:
  She _____
  and she _____ .
2 One thing she can do / one thing she can't do:
  She _____
  but she _____ .

6 ⭐ Write about you. Use *can* or *can't*.

1 I _____ swim.
2 I _____ water ski.
3 I _____ play the guitar.
4 I _____ sing.
5 I _____ dance.
6 I _____ climb.

7 ⭐⭐⭐ Write four sentences about you. Use *can* or *can't*.

_____
_____
_____
_____
_____
_____
_____
_____
_____
_____

Reading

8 Read the texts. True or false?

Monkey trouble

This is an orangutan from Sumatra. Sumatra is in Asia. Orangutans have got long red hair. They can climb and jump, but they can't fly!

This is a Capuchin monkey. It's from South America. It's small and thin and it's got white and black hair. It can jump and climb, but it can't swim.

1	Orangutans are from Asia.	*true*
2	Capuchin monkeys are from South America.	_____
3	Orangutans have got black hair.	_____
4	Orangutans have got short hair.	_____
5	Orangutans can climb and jump.	_____
6	Capuchin monkeys have got brown hair.	_____
7	Capuchin monkeys can jump.	_____
8	Capuchin monkeys can swim.	_____

9 Correct the false sentences.

1 *Orangutans haven't got black hair. They've got red hair.*
2 _____
3 _____
4 _____

1 Read about this robot toy. Answer true or false.

Gupi is amazing. He's small, he has got ears and feet and a mouth and eyes. He can listen to you, and he can talk. He can move and he can eat! Gupi's really fun!

1 Gupi has got ears.   *true*
2 He can listen.   _____
3 He has got a mouth.   _____
4 He can't talk.   _____
5 He has got eyes.   _____

Talking Tips!

2 Circle six Talking Tips.

3 Complete the dialogue. Use these words.

robot   can   animal   come on   no way

Ben Look at this robot, Felix.
Felix It's not a ¹ ***robot***! It's an animal!
Ben No, it isn't an ² _____ , it's a robot toy!
Felix Wow! It's great!
Ben Look, it can eat!
Felix No! ³ _____ !
Ben Yes, really. Look!
Felix Wow! It's amazing. ⁴ _____ it run?
Ben Yes, look!
Felix Hey! Where is it now? Hurry up, Ben!
⁵ _____ !

Body parts

4 Which animal do they come from?

1 It's got ***a dolphin's head.***
2 It's got _____
3 It's got _____
4 It's got _____
5 It's got _____

5 Write about you. Use these words.

hands   feet   arms   legs   nose   mouth

1 I've got _two hands._
2 I've got _____
3 I _____
4 _____
5 _____
6 _____

Can you …?

6 ⭐ Match the questions and answers.

1 Can we run?   a Yes, I can.
2 Can they fly?   b No, she can't.
3 Can she water ski?   c Yes, we can.
4 Can he paint?   d No, they can't.
5 Can I jump?   e Yes, he can.

7 ⭐ Complete the questions and answers. Use _can_ or or _can't_.

1 _Can_ you swim? Yes, I can.
2 Can Felix swim? No, he _____ .
3 _____ he sing? No, he _____ .
4 _____ Felix and Gemma play music?
   No, they _____ .
5 _____ Monica dance? Yes, she _____ .
6 _____ Gemma sing? No, she _____ .

8 ⭐⭐ Interview Gupi, the animal robot in Exercise 1. Then write his answers.

1 sing? ✗   _Can you sing?   No, I can't._
_____

2 talk? ✓   _____
_____

3 eat? ✓   _____
_____

4 run? ✓   _____
_____

5 jump? ✗   _____
_____

6 paint? ✗   _____
_____

7 walk? ✓   _____
_____

8 play the drums? ✗   _____
_____

9 ⭐⭐ Write questions and answers.

1 He / sing? ✓   _Can he sing?   Yes, he can._
_____

2 We / fly? ✗   _____
_____

3 They / move? ✓   _____
_____

4 You / water ski? ✓   _____
_____

5 She / climb? ✗   _____
_____

6 You / play the drums? ✓   _____
_____

7 He / paint pictures? ✗   _____
_____

1 Match the dialogues and the pictures.

①  ②

③  ④

a Mum, can I have a drink?
Yes, of course you can! _____
b Can we touch the giraffe?
No, you can't! _____
c Hello! Can I sit down here?
Yes, of course you can! _____
d Hello! Can we take a photo?
Yes, you can. _____

2 Order the words.

1 I the Can tiger touch ?
Can I touch the tiger?

2 you No can't .
_____

3 photos take I Can ?
_____

4 can you Yes .
_____

5 you talk Can ?
_____

6 we can Yes .
_____

Adjectives

3 Find these words in the word square.

~~big~~ great slow fast nice
long dangerous clever beautiful

S	B	H	B	I	V	S	R	P
F	E	R	I	E	G	L	Z	W
D	A	N	G	E	R	O	U	S
C	U	J	P	G	E	W	O	F
M	T	X	Y	D	A	R	F	C
N	I	C	E	D	T	X	L	K
W	F	A	S	T	Q	F	R	E
K	U	E	W	L	O	N	G	W
C	L	E	V	E	R	A	B	N

Asking for permission

4 Find three questions and answers in the spiral.

ofcourseyoucan.CanIopenthewindow?No,youcan't.CanIeatthis?Yes,youcan.Yes,ofcourseyoucan?Canwesitdownhere?

1 *Can we sit down here?*
2 _____ ?
3 _____ ?
4 _____
5 _____ ?
6 _____

5 Fill in the missing letters.

1 C _a_ n we s__t d__wn?
2 Ca__ __e t __ke ph __t __s?
3 Ca __ I s __ng a song?
4 C __n __e __ave a d __i __k?
5 C __n I __pen th __ wi __d __w?

6 Write questions asking for permission.

1 touch the dolphin   _Can I touch the dolphin?_
2 open the window
_____
3 take my MP3 player
_____
4 play music
_____
5 have a drink
_____
6 climb on a chair
_____
7 sit next to the dog
_____

7 Put the stickers in the correct place.

> Sticker

① These animals are great! They can't run and they can't fly, but they can jump! They've got big legs.

> Sticker

② These are funny animals! They can jump and they can climb. They've got long arms and they're orange.

8 Complete the report. Use these words.

are   take   Has   talk   they   ~~your~~

REPORT FROM OUTER SPACE

Hello Fiz!

Thank you for ¹_your_ report.
Please answer our questions.
What ²_____ parrots?
Can ³_____ talk?
Can we see the parrots? Can you
⁴_____ a photo?
⁵_____ Bandit got a big brother?
Can he ⁶_____ ? Is he dangerous?

Bye!

Your friends from outer space.

Fiz's Learning Blog

Remember words

Think of a funny picture to help you remember.

Reading

1 Read about these sharks from Australia. True or false?

This is the Wobbegong shark. It isn't beautiful – it's really ugly! It's got lots of teeth, it's long and it's big, but you can't see it. It's a brown colour. It's dangerous – don't swim next to the wobbegong!

Now here's a very ugly shark! Meet the Megamouth shark. It's a really BIG shark and it's got a really BIG mouth. The shark's body is black and white and it's got lots of small teeth. But it's OK – it can't eat you! It eats small things in the sea.

The Wobbegong

1 It's a beautiful shark.   *false*
2 It's a big shark.   _____
3 It isn't long.   _____
4 It hasn't got any teeth.   _____
5 It's red.   _____
6 It's dangerous.   _____

The Megamouth

 7 It's a beautiful shark.   _____
 8 It's black and white.   _____
 9 It's got lots of teeth.   _____
10 It eats big things in the sea. _____

Writing

2 Write about dolphins. Use these words.

> it's   it isn't   it has got   it hasn't got   it can   it can't

The **dolphin** Fact file

Size: small

Colour: blue, black and white. Beautiful.

Teeth: lots of teeth! (48–72)

Can: swim fast, jump

Can eat: small things in the sea

_____
_____
_____
_____
_____
_____
_____
_____
_____
_____

My Life

My Picture Dictionary

Routines

1 Label the pictures. Use these words.

study   walk to school   meet friends   have dinner
go to bed   watch TV   finish school   ~~get up~~

① *get up*

② _____

③ _____

④ _____

⑤ _____

⑥ _____

⑦ _____

⑧ _____

2 Find the words round the clock.

my words

Do you know more words to describe routines? Write them here.

_____
_____
_____
_____
_____

Time

1 Match the times and the clocks.

 ① ② ③

_b_ _____ _____ _____

 ④  ⑤

_____ _____

a It's one o'clock.
b It's eight o'clock.
c It's seven o'clock.
d It's nine o'clock.
e It's three o'clock.

2 Write the times.

 ① ② ③

 ④ ⑤ ⑥

1 It's **seven** o'clock.
2 It's _____
3 _____
4 _____
5 _____
6 _____

3 Complete the text. Use the verbs on page 31.

I ¹ **get up** at eight o'clock. I sing in the shower!
I ² _____ at nine o'clock.
We ³ _____ at four
o'clock and I ⁴ _____ .
I ⁵ _____ at six o'clock
and I ⁶ _____ .
I ⁷ _____
at eight o'clock and at ten o'clock I
⁸ _____ .

Talking Tips!

4 Circle two Talking Tips.

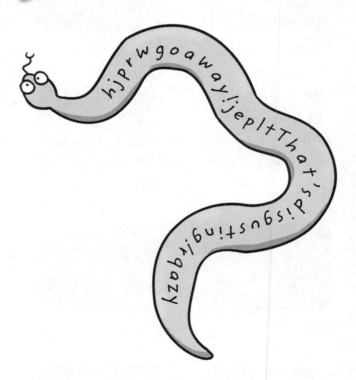

hjprwgoaway!jepltThax'sdisgusting!rgazy

5 Complete the dialogue. Use these Talking Tips.

> come on   That's disgusting   ~~What~~
> Go away

Felix	Gemma! Gemma!
Gemma	¹ *What* ?
Felix	Look!
Gemma	It's time to study, Felix. ² _____ !
Felix	Oh ³ _____ . Look at me! I'm an elephant!
Gemma	Oh, OK… Oh Felix! ⁴ _____ ! You've got bananas in your mouth. Now we can't eat them! It isn't funny.
Felix	Oh yes it is! Ha! Ha!

Present simple: affirmative

6 ☆ Circle the correct word.

1 Gemma **get** / **(gets up)** at seven o'clock.
2 Felix **eat** / **eats** breakfast at eight o'clock.
3 Ben **go** / **goes** to school at nine o'clock.
4 Monica **have** / **has** lunch at school.
5 Gemma **study** / **studies** after school.
6 Felix **watch** / **watches** TV after dinner.

7 ☆ Write the correct form.

1 I get up   He *gets up*
2 I go to bed   She _____
3 I have lunch   He _____
4 I watch TV   She _____
5 I study   He _____
6 I finish school   She _____

8 ☆ What's true for you? Circle the words.

1 I study at **school** / **in bed**.
2 I eat breakfast **at home** / **at school**.
3 I have lunch **at school** / **at home**.
4 I meet my friends **at school** / **after school**.
5 I watch TV **at school** / **at home**.
6 I go to bed at **7 o'clock**. / **late**.

9 ☆☆ Write about Ben.

> I get up at six o'clock.

1 Ben *gets up at six o'clock.*

> I have breakfast at seven o'clock.

2 He _____

> I go to school at nine o'clock.

3 He _____

> I meet my friends at three o'clock.

4 He _____ his _____

> I study at seven o'clock.

5 He _____

> I watch TV at eight o'clock.

6 He _____

Writing

10 Write about your day.

I _____ up at _____ o'clock.
I _____ breakfast at _____
_____ . I _____ to
school at _____ I finish school at
_____ . I _____ dinner
at _____ . I _____ to bed at
_____ .

Discover 5 extra words. Go to page 87.

Transport

1 Complete the puzzle.

> car   train   ~~bike~~   plane   motorbike   boat   bus

Reading

2 Read the texts and complete the sentences.

(a) Hi! I'm Ellie and I'm from New York in the USA. I go to school by boat — my school is on Staten Island.

(b) Hello, my name is Mathieu and I'm from France. I get up at seven o'clock on school days and I go to school by bike. All my friends have bikes too. We don't walk to school.

(c) Hi, I'm Maria and I'm from Greece. I don't walk to school — my school is far from my house. I go there by bus. I get up at six o'clock and the bus is here at seven o'clock.

(d) Hello, I'm Stephen and I'm from Australia. My home is far from school. I don't go to school, I study at home! But I've got lots of friends here. We all study at home.

1 Ellie goes to school by **_boat._**
2 Maria goes to school by _____
3 Mathieu goes to school by _____
4 Stephen doesn't go _____

5 Ellie is from _____
6 Mathieu gets up at _____
7 Maria doesn't _____ to school.

Present simple: negative

3 ☆ Read page 42 of the Students' Book again. These sentences are false. Correct them.

1 James goes to school by train.
James doesn't go to school by train.

2 Kim walks to school every day.
_____

3 She goes to school with her sister on Wednesday.
_____

4 Dakota walks to school.
_____

5 James' friends go to school by bike.
_____

6 Amit gets up at eight o'clock.
_____

4 ☆☆ Now write the correct sentences.

1 James go / bus
James goes to school by bus.

2 Kim walk / Monday
_____

3 She go / Tuesdays
_____

4 Dakota go / boat
_____

5 Amit go / bike
_____

6 Amit get up / six o'clock
_____

5 ☆☆ Write negative sentences.

1 we / not get up at 6 o'clock.
We don't get up at 6 o'clock.

2 I / not walk to school.
_____

3 they / not go by bus.
_____

4 we / not go by motorbike.
_____

5 My friends / not meet on Sunday.
_____

6 I / not go to bed at ten o'clock.
_____

Present simple: affirmative and negative

6 ☆ Look at the table and complete the sentences.

Transport to school

	Kylie	David	Jennie	Leon
go by bus	✓ Friday	✓	✗	✗
go by car	✗	✓ Monday, Friday	✓ Monday	✗
go by train	✗	✗	✓	✗
go by bike	✓	✗	✗	✗
walk	✗	✗	✗	✓

1 David usually goes to school by ***bus.***
2 Jennie ***doesn't go*** to school by bus.
3 Leon _____ to school.
4 Kylie _____ walk to school.
5 David goes to school by _____ on Mondays and Fridays.
6 Leon _____ to school by train.
7 Kylie usually _____ to school by bike.
8 Jennie _____ to school by car on Monday.

7 ☆☆ Write sentences about you.

1 go / school / car
I go to school by car. OR

I don't go to school by car.

2 walk / school
_____

3 meet my friends / the weekend
_____

4 live / London
_____

5 get up / 8 o'clock
_____

6 go / school / boat
_____

Earth Explorer

Present simple: questions

1 ⭐ Read the interview with Bandit and complete the factfile with ✓ (Yes) or ✗ (No).

Q Do you go to work?
Bandit No, I don't.
Q Do you live in a house?
Bandit Yes, I do.
Q Do you sleep in a bed?
Bandit Yes, I do.
Q Do you eat bats' legs?
Bandit No, I don't. That's disgusting!
Q Do you eat breakfast?
Bandit Yes, I do.
Q Have you got a toy mouse?
Bandit Yes, I have. It's Fiz!

Bandit:	
goes to work	✗
lives in a house	
sleeps in a bed	
eats bats' legs	
eats breakfast	
has got a toy mouse	

2 ⭐ Write *do* or *does*.

1 _Do_ they eat lunch at 1 o'clock?
2 _____ he study at home?
3 _____ you watch TV after dinner?
4 What time _____ you have breakfast?
5 What time _____ he get up?
6 _____ we go to school after breakfast?

3 ⭐⭐ Ask Kit questions.

1 live / in a house?
Do you live in a house?
2 Bandit / sleep in a bag?
_____
3 you / go to work?
_____
4 your mum / work?
_____
5 Bandit / eat bats' legs?
_____
6 Fiz / sleep in a bag?
_____

4 ⭐ Write questions with *What time ... ?*

1 What time / you get up?
What time do you get up?
2 What time / you go to bed?
_____
3 What time / Bandit eat lunch?
_____
4 What time / your mum start work?
_____
5 What time / we go to school?
_____
6 What time / they finish school?
_____

5 ⭐ Answer questions about you.

1 Do you live in a house? _____
2 Do you go to school? _____
3 What time do you get up? _____
4 What time do you finish school? _____
5 Do you have lunch at school? _____
6 What do you eat for breakfast? _____
7 Where do you live? _____

Time

6 Write the times.

① ② ③

④ ⑤ ⑥

1 It's ___half past___ eight.
2 It's _____ eleven.
3 It's _____
4 It's _____
5 It's _____
6 It's _____

7 Put the stickers in the correct place.

Sticker

① I'm Mikkina and I'm from Planet Kipkip. My planet is very cold. There are only eight hours in a day. We live in small houses in the sea, and we sleep in boats.

Sticker

② My name's Joyba and I'm from planet Froooo. My planet is very big and hot. We live and sleep in treehouses. There are fifty hours in a Froooo day.

8 Complete the report. Use these words.

hours   time   ~~you~~   What

REPORT FROM OUTER SPACE

Hello Fiz!

Thank ¹ **you** for your report. Please answer our questions.
² _____ do Earth people eat?
What ³ _____ do they sleep?
Are there seventy-two ⁴ _____ in an Earth day?
Have you got your spaceboard there?

Bye!

Your friends from outer space.

Fiz's Learning Blog

Remember words / verbs with times of day

My day

I get up at 7.00.
↓
I eat breakfast at 8.00.
↓
I go to school at 9.00.

4d Let's Revise!

Vocabulary

1 Write animals starting with:

1 g _____   3 t _____
2 m _____   4 s _____

2 Write action verbs starting with:

1 j _____   3 d _____
2 c _____   4 r _____

3 Find the parts of the body.

1 daeh _____   4 oet _____
2 umoht _____   5 seon _____
3 ginfre _____

4 Complete the words.

1 w __ __ k to sch __ __ l
2 h __ __ e din __ __ __
3 wa __ __ __ TV
4 m __ __ t fr __ __ __ __ s

5 Complete the sentences.

1 I go to school by b __ __ __.
2 I go to school by __ __ a t.
3 I go to school by __ r __ i n.
4 I go to school by __ __ s.

___/21

Grammar

6 Complete with *can / can't*.

1 Dolphins _____ swim.
2 Kangaroos _____ jump.
3 Elephants _____ dance.
4 Tigers _____ paint.

7 Circle the correct word.

1 Gemma **get / gets** up at 7.15.
2 Felix and Gemma **walk / walks** to school.
3 Gemma **study / studies** after school.

8 Write negative sentences.

1 I eat breakfast at 8.15.
_____

2 We walk to school.
_____

3 Monica finishes her homework on the bus.
_____

4 Ben sings on the bus.
_____

9 Complete the questions and answers.

1 _____ you start school at 9.00?
Yes, _____
2 _____ they eat cereal for breakfast?
No, _____
3 _____ Felix go to bed at 8.00?
No, _____
4 _____ Gemma live in a house?
Yes, _____

___/15

Functions

10 Write the times in words.

1 10.00 _____
2 6.15 _____
3 3.45 _____
4 8.15 _____

___/4

Your score	Your total score
	___/40

30–40   20–30   0–20

38

5 Sport

My Picture Dictionary

Sports

1 Label the pictures.

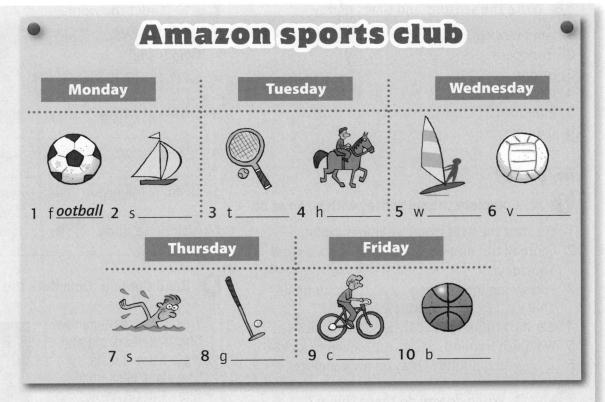

Amazon sports club

Monday

1 f _ootball_ 2 s_____ **Tuesday** 3 t_____ 4 h_____ **Wednesday** 5 w_____ 6 v_____

Thursday 7 s_____ 8 g_____ **Friday** 9 c_____ 10 b_____

2 Describe these sports.

	Volleyball	Cycling	Golf	Swimming
Water sport	✗	✗	✗	✓
Play with a ball	✓	✗	✓	✗

Volleyball
1 It _isn't_ a water sport.
2 I _play_ with a ball.

Cycling
3 It _____ a water sport.
4 I _____ _____ with a ball.

Golf
5 It _____ a water sport.
6 I _____ with a ball.

Swimming
7 It _____ a water sport.
8 I _____ _____ with a ball.

my words

Do you know more sports words? Write them here.

_____
_____
_____

Sports Heroes

Seasons and times of day

1 Write the seasons and times of day.

1 vengine **_evening_**
2 ftnnooera _____
3 ipsgnr _____
4 umautn _____
5 inmrong _____
6 meumsr _____

in, on, at

2 ☆ Complete the sentences with *in*, *on* or *at*.

1 We start the new school year **_in_** autumn.
2 Football training is _____ Tuesdays and Thursdays.
3 I do swimming training _____ summer. That's _____ Wednesday.
4 We start training _____ four o'clock.
5 We finish training _____ seven o'clock.
6 _____ Sunday I play on my computer.

3 ☆☆ When do *you* do these things?

1 eat dinner **_in the evening_**
2 your homework _____
3 have breakfast _____
4 meet friends _____
5 go to school _____
6 visit your granny and granddad
   _____
7 watch football _____

Present simple: questions

4 ☆ Order the words.

1 [is] [Who] [she] ?
   Who is she?
2 [is] [he from] [Where] ?
   _____
3 [do] [Where] [they] [play volleyball] ?
   _____
4 [they] [do] [When] [train] ?
   _____
5 [do] [they go] [on holiday] [When] ?
   _____
6 [favourite thing] [her] [is] [What] ?
   _____

5 Read the text. Complete the factfile.

This is Maria Stepanova. She's 28 years old and she's from Russia. She plays basketball. She's 2m 03. Wow! She's very tall! Maria plays basketball in Russia but she lives in the USA. Maria plays basketball and hockey too.

Maria trains every day and she has got a family. She is a mum and she has got a sister too. She likes music. Her favourite singer is Ricky Martin.

Name	¹ *Maria Stepanova*
Age	2
From	3
Sport	4
Lives	5
Trains	6
Likes	7

Reading

6 Read about Joe Mensah and answer the questions.

Who is he?
He's Francis Joe Mensah, and he's 15 years old.

Where is he from?
He's from Africa.

Where does he live?
He lives in Ghana.

Where does he play football?
He plays in the Feyenoord Fetteh Football Academy, in Ghana.

When does he train?
He trains in the afternoon, after school.

What does he do in the morning?
He has lessons.

What does he do in the evening?
He watches TV.

Does he go on holiday in summer?
No, he doesn't. He plays football every day.

1 What is his name?
Francis Joe Mensah

2 Is he American?
_____

3 Does he play football at school?
_____

4 Does he train after lessons?
_____

5 Does he play in the morning?
_____

6 What does he do in the evening?
_____

7 What does he do in summer?
_____

7 Read about these sports stars. Complete the questions and answers.

Amelie Mauresmo

1 *What* does she play? She plays *tennis*.

2 _____ her favourite colour? It's _____

3 _____ does she meet her friends?
On _____

Tiger Woods

4 _____ is he from? He's from _____

5 _____ is his sport? His sport is _____

6 _____ does he play golf? He plays golf
_____ _____

Amelie Mauresmo
I play tennis. It's my sport. I'm from France. I'm tall and I've got long hair. My favourite colour is blue. On Saturday I meet friends and on Sunday I sleep!

Tiger Woods
I'm from the USA. My sport is golf. I play golf every day. My favourite colour is green. I don't like swimming but I like tennis.

---

8 ⭐⭐ Answer the questions about you. Write complete sentences.

1 When do you play on the computer?
I play _____

2 Where do you live?
I live _____

3 Who is your favourite sports star?
_____

4 What time do you eat breakfast?
_____

5 When do have fun with your friends?
_____

6 Who is at home on Sunday?
_____

go and play

1 ☆ Write *go* or *play*.

1 *play* volleyball
2 _____ swimming
3 _____ tennis
4 _____ windsurfing
5 _____ football
6 _____ golf
7 _____ horse riding
8 _____ basketball

2 ☆ Complete the sentences. Use *play*, *plays*, *go* or *goes*.

1 Gemma **goes** horse riding.
2 She _____ tennis too.
3 She doesn't _____ football.
4 Felix _____ football.
5 Ben _____ swimming.
6 Ben doesn't _____ dancing.

3 ☆☆ What sports do you do? Write sentences.

1 tennis
   I play tennis.
2 swimming
   I don't go swimming.
3 basketball
   _____
4 volleyball
   _____
5 horse riding
   _____
6 golf
   _____
7 football
   _____

4 ☆ Read the interview with Niki, from Greece. Write what she does at the times in the table.

Q Niki, you do lots of things every Saturday.
A Yes, I do. I have my music lesson at 9 o'clock in the morning. I like playing music. After the lesson I go horse riding. That's my favourite.
Q What do you do in the afternoon?
A I play tennis at 1 o'clock and I go dancing at 3 o'clock. I go home at 5 o'clock and I sit down!
Q And in the evening?
A I stop! I play with my computer and I watch TV!

Time	What does Niki do?
9.00 – 10.00	¹ *She has her music lesson.*
10.00 – 12.00	²
1.00 – 3.00	³
3.00 – 5.00	⁴
5.00 – (3 things)	⁵

5 ☆☆ What do you do on Saturday at these times?

1 In the morning I _____
2 In the afternoon I _____
3 In the evening I _____

6 ☆☆☆ Write about you and your friend.

1 What do you do on Sunday? *On Sunday I*
   _____

2 What does your friend do on Sunday?
   On Sunday she / he
   _____

Talking Tips!

7 Circle two Talking Tips.

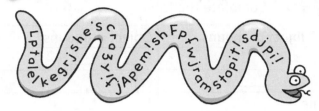

8 Meet the Acro Bats! Read the dialogue and complete the sentences.

| stop | doing | ~~on~~ | crazy | way |

– Come ¹*on* ! Climb on!
– No ² _____ !
– But it's fun!
– No, it isn't. You're ³ _____ ! It's dangerous!
– Oh ⁴ _____ it! I love ⁵ _____ this!
– Well, you do it! I hate it!
– Is your name Acro Bat? We are the Acro Bat family!
– No, I'm just Bat!

like + -ing

9 ☆ Write the *–ing* forms of these verbs.

1 play   *playing*
2 sail   _____
3 dance   _____
4 go   _____
5 swim   _____
6 run   _____
7 ride   _____
8 do   _____

10 ☆☆ Write sentences.

1 I like / swim. *I like swimming.*
2 Felix hate / run. _____
3 I / not like / paint. _____
4 Gemma love / dance. _____
5 Felix/ not like / sing. _____
6 Ben hate /go sailing. _____

11 ☆ Answer the questions about you.

1 Do you like windsurfing? *Yes, I do. / No, I don't.*
2 Do you like running? _____
3 Do you like swimming? _____
4 Does your dad like climbing? _____
5 Does your mum like swimming? _____
6 What do you like doing on holiday? _____

12 ☆☆ Complete. Use *do, does, doing,* or *doesn't*.

1 *Do* you like sailing? Yes, I *do* .
2 What _____ you like _____ on Sunday? I like watching TV.
3 _____ he like climbing? No, he _____
4 _____ she like running? Yes, she _____
5 What sport _____ he like _____ ? He loves windsurfing.

Object pronouns

1 ⭐ Answer the questions about the Earth Explorer cartoon. Use these words.

> a camera   David Becker   a zapper

Kit:	Have you got **it**?
Mindy:	Yes, I have… oh, where is **it**?
Kit:	Come on!
Mindy:	OK, OK… ah! Here **it** is.
Kit:	Give it to me. Let's take a photo.

1 What is **it**? _____

Kit:	Look at **him**! He's fast!
Mindy:	Oh yes, he is. I like **him**!
Kit:	He scores lots of goals. Yeah! GOAL!
Mindy:	Great! Now I really like **him**!

2 Who is **him**? _____

Fiz:	I don't like this sport.
Kit:	What? Football? But it's great!
Fiz:	No, no, let's stop the game. Now, where is **it**?
Kit:	Fiz! Don't!
Fiz:	Come on! Let's use **it**! Hee! Hee! (ZAP!)
Kit:	Oh no …

3 What is **it**? _____

2 ⭐ Complete the table.

Subject pronouns	Object pronouns
I	3 _____
1 _____	you
he	4 _____
she	5 _____
it	it
we	6 _____
2 _____	them

3 ⭐⭐ Complete the tables.

Subject pronouns	Object pronouns	Possessive adjectives
1 _____	me	8 _____
you	4 _____	9 _____
he	5 _____	his
2 _____	her	10 _____
3 _____	6 _____	its
we	us	11 _____
they	7 _____	12 _____

4 ⭐ Write object pronouns.

1 **He** is great. I love *him.*
2 **She's** crazy. I like _____
3 This is my new **football**. Can you see _____ ?
4 They are a good **team**. Do you like _____ ?
5 **We** are at the match. Can you see _____ ?
6 I'm with Mindy. She's with _____

5 ⭐⭐ Rewrite the sentences. Use object pronouns.

1 I like David Becker. I *like him.*
2 Fiz has got the zapper. Fiz _____
3 Mindy has got the camera. _____
4 Fiz can't see the match. _____
5 Kit's got Fiz in the bag. _____ the bag.
6 We like playing football. _____

Making suggestions

6 Order the words.

1 [home] [Let's] [go] .
Let's go home.

2 [How about] [basketball] [playing] ?
_____

3 [eat] [lunch] [Let's] .
_____

4 [go] [Let's] [running] .
_____

5 [going to] [the match] [How about] ?
_____

6 [going] [How about] [windsurfing] ?
_____

7 [Let's] [swimming] [go] .
_____

7 Put the stickers in the correct place.

> **Sticker**

① **What's my sport?**
I love doing this sport. I don't play with a ball and it isn't a water sport. I do the sport with an animal and we run and jump very fast.

> **Sticker**

② **What's my sport?**
This is my favourite sport. We go really fast! There are four people in my team and we do our sport on the water. It's really fun!

8 Complete the report. Use these words.

> sharks ~~sports~~ Bye run ball swim

REPORT FROM OUTER SPACE

Hello Fiz!
Thank you for your report.
They've got funny ¹**sports** on Earth.
They ²_____ in the sea! They play with a ³_____ ! They do sports with horses!
On our planet we ⁴_____ with turtles. We love turtle running. And we go windsurfing with ⁵_____
That's great! Can you do sharksurfing on Earth?
⁶_____ !

Your friends from outer space.

Fiz's Learning Blog

Remember grammar

Repeat words and phrases like a song!

Object pronouns chant

Me and you and him and her

It and us and them!

–ing chant

I love swimming   I hate swimming

I like swimming   And I love singing this!

45

1 Label the photos.

> swimming   face painting   playing football
> singing   ~~painting~~   playing tennis

①
painting

②
_____

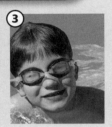
③
_____

④
_____

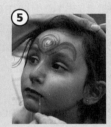
⑤
_____

⑥
_____

Reading

2 Read the text and answer the questions.

How about a summer holiday at Super Camp?

Do you like swimming and playing football? How about riding a bike? You can do all these things and there's tennis, and painting and face painting! There's horse riding and basketball too.

In the evening you can dance and sing!

1 Can you go swimming at Super Camp?
   Yes, you can.
2 Can you play tennis?
   _____
3 Have they got bikes at Super Camp?
   _____
4 What do people do in the evening?
   _____

3 Complete this poster for Super Camp.

Super Camp Holidays

Morning activities
t _e n n i s_
sw __ __ __ __ __ __
horse ri __ __ __ __
foo __ __ __ __ __

Aft __ __ __ __ __ __ activities
painting
face p __ __ __ __ __ __ __
cyc __ __ __ __
bask __ __ __ __ __ __

Ev __ __ __ __ __ activities
dan __ __ __ __
si __ __ __ __ __

For children 4–13 years old

Come for 7 days or 14 days. It's great fun!

4 What can you do at Super Camp?

Morning
You can _____
You _____
_____
_____

Afternoon
You can _____
You _____
_____
_____

Evening
You can _____
You _____
_____
_____

My Picture Dictionary

Places in town

1 Label the picture.

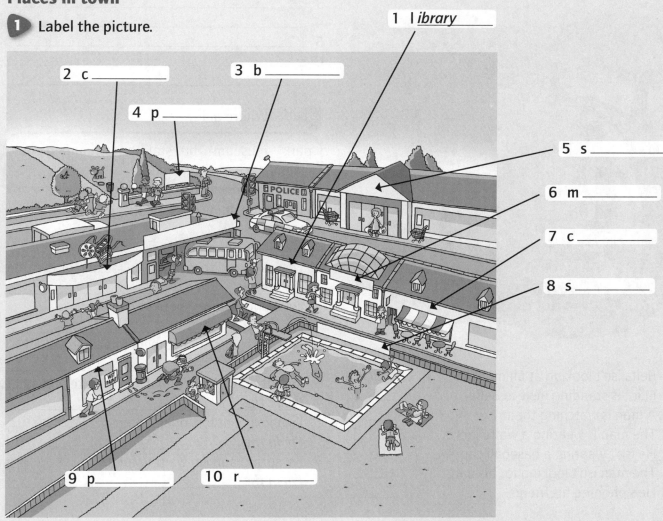

1   l *ibrary*

2   c _____

3   b _____

4   p _____

5   s _____

6   m _____

7   c _____

8   s _____

9   p _____

10 r _____

2 Where do you go:

1   for a bus?   *bus station*
2   for a drink?   _____
3   to go swimming?   _____
4   for books?   _____
5   to see a film?   _____
6   for a walk?   _____
7   for food?   _____

my words

Do you know more town words?
Write them here.

_____
_____
_____

Present continuous: affirmative and negative

1 ☆ Look at the picture and read the sentences. True or false?

1	Bella isn't looking at Elliot.	*false*
2	Elliot is standing next to Bella.	_____
3	A man is watching them.	_____
4	The man is wearing a white jacket.	_____
5	He isn't wearing a baseball cap.	_____
6	The man isn't looking for his bag.	_____
7	He's phoning his friend.	_____

2 ☆ Complete the table.

I	_'m_	talking	at the moment.
1 _____	're	sitting.	
He	4 _____	walking	now.
2 _____	's	running.	
It	5 _____	stopping	now.
We	6 _____	talking	at the moment.
3 _____	're	smiling.	

3 ☆☆ Make the sentences in the table negative.

1 *I'm not talking at the moment.*
2 _____
3 _____
4 _____
5 _____
6 _____
7 _____

4 ☆ Where am I?

park   museum   bus station   swimming pool
cinema   ~~classroom~~   café

1 I'm sitting at my desk. I'm listening to the teacher.
I'm in the classroom.
2 I'm walking with my dog. I'm looking at the trees.
I'm in the _____
3 I'm doing a water sport with my friends.
I'm in the _____
4 I'm sitting at a small table. I'm having a drink.
I'm in the _____
5 I'm sitting with my friend. We're watching a film.
I'm in the _____
6 I'm looking at lots of old things.
I'm in the _____
7 I'm sitting and I'm waiting for a bus.
I'm in the _____

5 ⭐⭐ Order the words.

1 dog | is running | The | to the trees .
The dog is running to the trees.
2 children | The | in the park | are walking .
_____
3 I | on TV | watching a film | am. .
_____
4 black jacket | The thief | a | is wearing .
_____
5 is listening to | his MP3 player | My friend .
_____
6 red bag | my | looking for | I am .
_____

6 ⭐ Write the *-ing* form of the words.

1 go   *going*
2 run   _____
3 stop   _____
4 look   _____
5 smile   _____
6 walk   _____
7 wear   _____
8 take   _____

7 ⭐ Complete the sentences. Use these words.

> is wearing   are following   is taking   are going
> is talking   ~~are looking~~   are wearing

1 The police *are looking* for three men.
2 Two men _____ black baseball caps.
3 The third man _____ a red baseball cap.
4 A girl _____ to the police in the park.
5 Two boys _____ to the police station.
6 The police _____ two young men.
7 A policeman _____ a man to the police station.

8 ⭐⭐ Complete the story. Use the present continuous of the verbs in brackets.

DJ — Here is the news. The police ¹*are looking* (look) for two men. One man is tall and has got black hair. His friend has got brown hair and ²_____ (wear) a baseball cap. The two thieves ³_____ (wear) jeans. Now here is Bob Mayhem. He ⁴_____ (talk) to the police.

Bob — Who are these men?

Police Officer — We ⁵_____ (look) for two thieves and they have got two big bags of money. Look! There they are!

Bob — Oh, yes, look! The policeman ⁶_____ (run) to the bus station. And the two men ⁷_____ (run) to the bus. Yes, they're on the bus now! Stop them!

9 ⭐ Read the sentences. Which are true for you? Correct the false sentences.

1 I am sitting in the kitchen at the moment.
_____
2 I am not sitting in the kitchen at the moment.
_____
3 I am studying English now.
_____
4 I am smiling at the moment.
_____

10 ⭐⭐⭐ Write true sentences about you *at the moment / now / today*.

1 listen *I am listening to music at the moment.*
2 sit   _____
3 talk   _____
4 smile _____
5 run   _____
6 open   _____
7 study _____

6ᵇ Is He Famous?

1 What are they doing? Complete the sentences.

look (x 2)   talk   read   have   ~~sit~~   eat

1 The children **_are sitting_** at a table.
2 'Daniel Craig' _____ on a mobile phone.
3 Felix _____ a drink.
4 Monica _____ a magazine.
5 She _____ at Felix.
6 Ben _____ a sandwich.
7 Gemma _____ at 'Daniel Craig'.

2 These sentences are false. Correct them.

1 The man is wearing a white T-shirt.
   The man isn't wearing a white T-shirt.
   He's wearing a black T- shirt.
2 Ben is having a drink.
   _____
   _____
3 Gemma is talking to the man.
   _____
   _____
4 Monica is looking at Ben.
   _____
   _____
5 Felix is eating a sandwich.
   _____
   _____
6 The man is listening to his MP3 player.
   _____
   _____
7 Gemma is sitting at the table.
   _____
   _____

3 A word in each sentence is mixed up. Can you work it out?

1 Daniel Craig is MASOUF   _**famous**_
2 Daniel is wearing a STTIRH   _**T-**_____
3 He is wearing EJSNA too.   _**j**_____
4 He's talking on his BOMELI phone.   _**m**_____
5 The children have got Daniel Craig's GRAUPHTOA   _**a**_____

Talking Tips!

4 Find two Talking Tips in the puzzle.

W	E	L	Z	F	J	R	P	J	U	H	I	L	A	C
H	O	W	E	M	B	A	R	R	A	S	S	I	N	G
P	S	T	U	C	R	O	P	I	A	T	T	U	O	N
A	R	I	Y	O	U	R	E	J	O	K	I	N	G	V
C	K	R	U	D	P	O	S	W	X	I	N	G	S	R
X	Q	B	A	Y	R	S	S	T	I	L	P	O	N	Q
V	F	Y	E	A	I	H	X	T	O	S	N	A	K	R
L	M	S	A	H	R	V	W	Q	U	J	O	W	B	X
C	H	A	U	G	Q	I	L	B	X	Y	P	M	T	S
B	F	E	N	Z	D	K	E	P	G	J	I	B	D	P
A	T	W	G	P	S	W	L	D	Y	X	B	Q	I	O

5 Complete the dialogue between Felix, Ben and Monica. Use these Talking Tips.

> How embarrassing   You're joking
> ~~Come on~~   Stop it

Monica, Ben, Gemma and Felix are having a drink in a café.

Gemma	Look it's 5 o'clock! [1]***Come on***, let's go.
Felix	Have you got any money?
Gemma	No I haven't, but Monica has got some money.
Monica	No, I haven't.
Gemma	Oh, Monica, [2]_____ !
Monica	No, I'm not joking. Ben, have you got any money?
Ben	No, I haven't.
Monica	What can we do? [3]_____ !
Ben / Felix	Ha! Ha!
Monica	Why are you laughing?
Gemma	Yes, you two. [4]_____ ! Don't laugh.
Ben	Your face! Ha! Ha! Of course we've got some money. Look!
Monica	You're terrible!

Clothes

6 Write the words.

1 *Jumper*   4 _____
2 _____   5 _____
3 _____   6 _____

7 ☆ Describe what these people are wearing today.

1 your sister or brother
   My sister is wearing jeans, a white top and brown boots.

2 your mum
   _____

3 your dad
   _____

4 your granddad
   _____

5 your friend
   _____

Present continuous: questions

8 ☆☆ Order the words. Write the answers.

1 today │ is your friend │ What │ doing │ ?
   What is your friend doing today?
   She is ...

2 you wearing │ are │ at the moment │ What │ ?
   _____
   _____

3 your mum │ Is │ at the moment │ eating │ ?
   _____
   _____

4 Is │ now │ reading a newspaper │ your dad │ ?
   _____
   _____

5 studying English │ Are │ today │ your friends │ ?
   _____
   _____

Directions

1 ☆ **Match the dialogues and the maps.**

1 Excuse me, where's the police station?
Go past the cinema and turn right. It's on your left. **_b_**

2 Excuse me, where's the bus station?
Go past the park, straight on and turn left.
The bus station's on your right. _____

3 Excuse me, where's the Post Office?
Go straight on past the supermarket. It's on the right. _____

4 Excuse me, where's the swimming pool?
Go straight on and turn right. It's past the library, on your left. _____

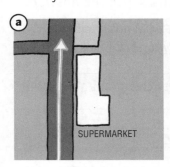
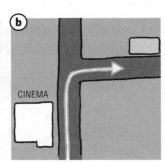
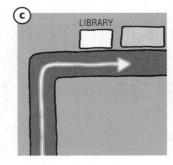
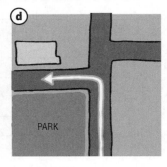

2 ☆ **Complete the phrases. Use _at_, _past_ or _on_.**

1 **_On_** the right.
2 Go straight _____ .
3 _____ your left.
4 Go _____ the Post Office.
5 Turn left _____ the park.

3 ☆☆ **Complete the dialogues. Use these words.**

past ~~on~~ on at on the right

Excuse me, I'm looking for the supermarket.
Go straight ¹**_on_** , ²_____ the library. Then turn right. The supermarket is ³_____ the left.

Excuse me, where is the park, please?
Turn left ⁴_____ the Post Office, then go straight ⁵_____ .Turn right. The park is on ⁶_____ .

4 ☆☆ **Write directions from the bus station to:**

1 the post office.
Go straight on… _____
_____

2 the park
_____
_____

3 the swimming pool
_____
_____

4 the supermarket
_____
_____

5 the café
_____
_____

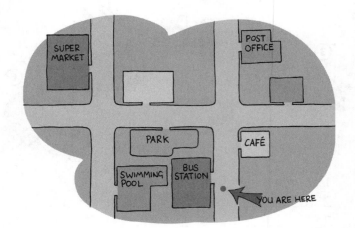

5 ⭐⭐ Write directions from your classroom to two places in your school. Choose from:

> the front door   the toilet   the teachers' room
> the café   the library   the computer room

_____
_____
_____
_____
_____

6 Put the correct sticker next to the description.

> **Sticker**

The police are looking for a thief. He is a young man and he is wearing a green baseball cap and a white T-shirt. He has got short black hair and brown eyes.

7 Put the other sticker here and complete the description. Use these words.

> T-shirt   long   eyes   ~~old~~   baseball cap

> **Sticker**

The police are looking for a thief. He is an ¹**old** man, and he is wearing a black ²_____ He isn't wearing a ³_____ He has got ⁴_____ brown hair and blue ⁵_____

8 Complete the report. Use these words.

> are   wearing   ~~What~~   looking   playing

REPORT FROM OUTER SPACE

Hello Fiz!

Thank you for your report.
We can see you on our spacevision.
¹**What** are you doing?
Are you ²_____ detectives?
Why ³_____ you acting?
This is very funny. We are ⁴_____ at peoples' clothes. What is Kit ⁵_____ today?

Your friends from outer space.

Fiz's Learning Blog

Remember words

Remember clothes words with parts of the body. Fill in the missing clothes words here.

Head: hat, baseball cap
Arms: top, T-shirt
Legs: trousers, _____
Feet: socks, _____

Remember! Clothes for your legs or for your feet have 2 parts, so they are PLURAL in English.

shoes   socks   boots   trousers   jeans

Examples
My boots are brown.
My trousers are blue.

Let's Revise!

Vocabulary

1 Complete the sports.

1 cy __ __ ing 3 v __ __ __ __ __ ball
2 sai __ __ __ g 4 ho __ __ e r __ d __ __ g

2 Write the seasons.

1 _____
2 _____
3 _____
4 _____

3 *Go* or *play*?

1 _____ swimming 3 _____ football
2 _____ tennis 4 _____ windsurfing

4 Complete the place words.

1 b __ s st __ __ __ __ n 3 cin __ __ __
2 p __ __ k 4 sup __ __ __ __ __ __ t

__/16

Grammar

5 Write *in*, *on* or *at*.

1 _____ the evening 3 _____ six o'clock
2 _____ Saturday 4 _____ autumn

6 Complete the questions. Write *When*, *Who*, *What* or *Where*.

1 _____ do you live? In London.
2 _____ is he? That's Franco.
3 _____'s your favourite sport? Tennis.
4 _____ do you go to school? In the morning.

7 Write the sentences using the present continuous of the verb in brackets.

1 Mick _____ (read) a magazine.
2 Brad _____ (run) with his dog.
3 The thieves _____ (open) a bag.
4 The police _____ (talk) to the thieves now.

8 Make present continuous questions with the words.

1 Felix / wear / boots?
   _____
2 Monica / wear / a T-shirt?
   _____
3 What / Gemma / wear/ today?
   _____
4 Gemma and Monica / write / the webpage today?
   _____

__/16

Functions

9 Make suggestions. Use *Let's* or *How about …?*

1 _____ go to the beach.
2 _____ going to a film?
3 _____ playing volleyball?
4 _____ have a drink.

10 Complete the directions.

A Excuse me, where is the cinema?
B Go ¹_____ on, then ²_____ right.
   Go ³_____ the library, the cinema is
   ⁴_____ the right.

__/8

Your score	Your total score
	__/40
30–40 20–30 0–20	

7 Celebrations

My Picture Dictionary

Months

1 Write the months.

Easter

Chinese New Year

Calendar 2010

January

_____
_____
_____
_____
_____
_____
_____
_____
_____
_____
_____

December

Hallowe'en

Christmas

2 Write the month.

Birthdays

When is your friend's birthday?
_____

When is your mum's birthday?
_____

When is your dad's birthday?
_____

When is your granddad's birthday?
_____

When is your granny's birthday?
_____

Holidays

Which month is Easter in your country?
_____

Which months do people go on holiday in your country?
_____,
_____,
_____

my words

Do you know more celebration words? Write them here.

_____
_____
_____
_____
_____

1 Circle the odd one out.

1 CD player	radio	(cake)	MP3 player
2 party	cake	sandwiches	pizza
3 present	card	party	café
4 football	T-shirt	tennis	basketball

2 Make phrases using a word from column A and words from column B.

A	B
buy	a card
open	a present
dance to	a birthday cake
listen to	a party
eat	a CD
have	music

1 BUY   *buy a card, buy a present,*
2 OPEN   _____
3 DANCE TO   _____
4 LISTEN TO   _____
5 EAT   _____
6 HAVE   _____

Talking Tips!

3 Find six Talking Tips in the birthday banners.

1 _____
2 _____
3 _____
4 _____
5 _____
6 _____

4 Complete the dialogue.

> That isn't fair   That's disgusting!   ~~Come on~~
> It's a joke   That's a good idea

Gemma   OK, now we've got Ben's present.
           [1]**Come on** , let's go to the café.
Monica   Brilliant! [2]_____ , I love the ice
           creams there.

At the café…
Gemma   Do you like your ice cream, Monica?
Monica   Mmmm, yes. It's great! And you?
Gemma   Yes, it's really good. What's that in your
           ice cream, Monica? Is it chocolate?
Monica   Chocolate? No… I haven't got chocolate.
           Oh! It's a bee! Uuugh.
           [3]_____ ! I can't eat that now!
Gemma   Oh, Monica it isn't a real bee! It's a toy!
Monica   Hmm. Why have I got a toy in my ice
           cream? Gemma?
Gemma   Ha! Ha! [4]_____ !
Monica   It isn't funny, Gemma. So, let's eat your
           ice cream!
Gemma   Hey! [5]_____ . Now I haven't got an
           ice cream.

Frequency adverbs

5 ☆ Find the adverbs of frequency.

1 veenr *never*   4 lulsayu _____
2 ftone _____   5 meessotim _____
3 wyasla _____

MOVE OVER!

THAT'S NOT FAIR!

THAT'S A GOOD IDEA!

HAPPY BIRTHDAY!

YOU'RE JOKING!

GO AWAY!

6 ☆ Complete the sentences using information in the table.

	always	usually	often	sometimes	never
have a party at Christmas	Teresa Apolonia	Marcos	Inigo		
go on holiday in the summer	Apolonia Teresa	Marcos			Inigo
go to school by bus	Teresa Inigo Marcos	Apolonia			
play basketball after school			Inigo Marcos	Teresa	Apolonia

1 Inigo **_often has_** a party at Christmas.
2 Teresa and Apolonia _____ _____ at Christmas.
3 Marcos _____ _____ Christmas.
4 Marcos _____ _____ in the summer.
5 Inigo _____ _____ in the summer.
6 Teresa, Inigo and Marcos _____ _____ by bus.

7 ☆☆ Put the adverb of frequency in the correct place. Write the sentences.

1 We go to the football match at the weekend. OFTEN
We often go to the football match at the weekend.
2 I listen to rock music. NEVER

_____

3 My sister listens to pop music on her MP3 player. OFTEN

_____

4 We have a party for my birthday. SOMETIMES

_____

5 I get lots of presents on my birthday. USUALLY

_____

6 I remember my friends' birthdays. ALWAYS

_____

8 ☆☆☆ Write similar sentences about you and your friends.

**I never have a party at Christmas.**

_____

_____

_____

_____

1 Find the words.

1 On my birthday I like eating KACSE. _cakes_
2 Easter Sunday is a ESAPILC day in many countries. _____
3 My MYLAIF celebrates Christmas in our house. _____
4 Lots of people have red SGEG at Easter. _____
5 We put our eggs in a KATBES. _____
6 Every RYAE there is a carnival in Brazil. _____
7 Chinese people make GOSDANR for the New Year celebration._____
8 In Poland people throw TRAWE at everyone at Easter. _____

Present simple and present continuous

2 ☆ Circle the correct words.

1 People usually **are celebrating** / ⟨**celebrate**⟩ Carnival in February.
2 Today I **am going** / **go** to the shops for presents.
3 Dorota **is having** / **has** lunch with her family every Christmas.
4 At the moment a man **is playing** / **plays** the drums.
5 I usually **am sending** / **don't send** cards at Easter.
6 Every Christmas we **are phoning** / **phone** our cousins in Australia.

3 ☆ Complete Jodie's letter to her friend Anna. Use these words.

> are eating   go   'm watching   eat
> 's swimming   is   have   ~~'m sitting~~

Dear Anna,

I ¹ **'m sitting** in my uncle's garden in Australia. We are here for our Christmas holiday. I ² _____ my brother Harry. He ³ _____ in the pool. Fantastic!

In Australia, Christmas is different from the UK: the weather ⁴ _____ usually very hot! They have summer in December in Australia. They never ⁵ _____ snow at Christmas. People often ⁶ _____ swimming on Christmas Day.

Christmas food in Australia is sometimes different too. People ⁷ _____ food from different countries like Italy, Spain, China, Japan and South America.

Today we are having an English Christmas lunch and we ⁸ _____ in the garden by the pool.

Have a good Christmas in the UK!

Love,

Jodie

4 ⭐⭐ **Complete the text with the present simple or the present continuous of the verbs in brackets.**

Hello, my name ¹ **is** (be) Jens. I ² _____ (be) from Denmark. I ³ _____ (love) Christmas. We ⁴ _____ (celebrate) it every year with the family. We ⁵ _____ (eat) lots of fish, and Mum and Dad ⁶ _____ (drink) special wine.

Today my Dad ⁷ _____ (buy) our Christmas tree. Every year we ⁸ _____ (have) the tree in the garden, and we ⁹ _____ (dance) around it in the days *before* Christmas.

At the moment I ¹⁰ _____ (write) cards and ¹¹ _____ (make) presents. I always ¹² _____ (make) my presents – cakes and special Christmas food.

5 ⭐⭐⭐ **Write four sentences about you and your family.**

1 What is your mum doing at the moment?
_____
_____

2 What is your dad doing at the moment?
_____
_____

3 What are you doing at the moment?
_____
_____

4 What do you do every day at school? Write three things.
_____
_____

Ordinal numbers

6 **Write the missing numbers and words.**

1st	¹ *first*	8th	⁵ _____
2nd	² _____	⁶ ___ ninth	
3rd	³ _____	12th	⁷ _____
⁴ ___ fourth			

7 **Look at the calendar and write the dates.**

DECEMBER

MON	TUE	WED	THURS	FRI	SAT	SUN
1 maths test	2 English test	3	4 Spanish test	5	6	7
8	9	10	11 Mum's birthday	12	13	14
15	16	17 Christmas party at school	18	19	20 Christmas holiday starts!	21
22	23	24	25 Christmas Day	26	27	28
29	30	31 New Year's Eve party				

1 When is Christmas Day?
   25th December
2 When is mum's birthday?
_____
3 When is the maths test?
_____
4 When does the Christmas holiday start?
_____
5 When is the Christmas party at school?
_____
6 When is the Spanish test?
_____

Earth Explorer

Weather

1 Read about the weather in these eight countries and draw weather symbols.

WORLD WEATHER

	Country	Weather	morning	afternoon
1	Australia	hot and sunny all day		
2	Brazil	sunny in the morning and cloudy in the afternoon		
3	Finland	cold and snowing all day		
4	France	foggy in the morning but sunny in the afternoon.		
5	Poland	raining in the morning and cloudy in the afternoon		
6	Portugal	sunny all day		
7	Greece	hot in the morning, cloudy in the afternoon		
8	Turkey	raining in the morning, but sunny in the afternoon		

2 Look at the tables and answer the questions.

The weather in Europe
Key:

H = hot	S = sunny
C = cold	CL = cloudy
F = foggy	R = raining
SN = snowing	W = windy

Belarus	SN
France	F, CL
Greece	H, S
Poland	CL, R
Portugal	H, R
Spain	S, H
Turkey	C, CL
UK	R, C

What's the weather like in:

1 the UK?   *It's raining and it's cold.*
2 Portugal? _____
3 Poland? _____
4 Greece? _____
5 Spain? _____
6 Belarus? _____
7 Turkey? _____
8 France? _____

3 What's the weather like in your country today?

_____
_____
_____
_____
_____
_____
_____
_____

4 Put the stickers in the correct place.

① This is my costume for Hallowe'en. It's long and white and it has got some purple in it. I haven't got a hat. I have got an orange pumpkin in my hand!

Sticker

② Do you like my Hallowe'en costume? It's very long and it's black. I've got a tall hat. My hair is long and black too with some white! I've got a long broom in my hand.

Sticker

5 Complete the report. Use these words.

planet   sunny   home   clothes   spooky   ~~cold~~

REPORT FROM OUTER SPACE

Hello Fiz!

Thank you for your report.

It is sometimes ¹*cold* on Earth – this is not good for aliens. On our ²_____ the weather is always hot and ³_____ .

What is Hallowe'en? You say it is ⁴_____ . What is spooky? Is this word like 'scary'? Why are costumes spooky? They are ⁵_____ !

Are you OK on Earth? Are you coming ⁶_____ , Fiz?

Your friends from outer space.

Fiz's Learning Blog

Remember words and grammar

Write sentences about YOU.
Examples
Dates
My birthday is on 4th March.
My sister's birthday is on October 1st.
My friend's party is on September 24th.

Adverbs of frequency/present simple
I always get up at 7 o'clock.
I never go to school on Sunday.
I often go swimming.

Directions to my school:
Go straight on and turn left.
Go past the park and it's on your right.

Discover **5** extra words. Go to page 87.

7ᵈ Festivals

Reading

1 Read Daniel's diary. Answer the questions.

August 30th

Today I'm at Notting Hill Carnival in London. It's great! People are celebrating Carnival in London! They celebrate the carnival every year, in August. The weather is fantastic today. It's usually hot and sunny in summer in London.

I'm listening to music at the moment – bands are playing in the street. Every year there are lots of bands. They all wear costumes and they play drums and guitars.

There is always lots of different food at the Carnival. I'm eating a big sandwich at the moment and I'm drinking a big cola! I can see lots of people and they are wearing costumes. They are singing and dancing in the street. I never sing and dance in the street! But my sister loves dancing and she wears special clothes every year.

1 In Daniel's diary, what are people doing today?
They're celebrating Carnival.

2 What do people do every year in London?
_____

3 What's the weather usually like?
_____

4 What is Daniel doing at the moment? (Write three things)
_____
_____

5 What do the bands play every year?
_____

6 What are people wearing?
_____

7 Does Daniel sing and dance in the street?
_____

Writing

2 Imagine you are at a festival in your country. Answer these questions.

1 Where are you?
In my house / in the street.

2 What month is it?
_____

3 What is the name of the festival?
_____

4 What are you doing at the moment?
_____

5 What do people usually do at this festival?
_____

6 What are you eating or drinking at the moment?
_____

3 Now use your answers to write about your festival. Use Daniel's diary to help you.
_____
_____
_____
_____
_____
_____

My Picture Dictionary

School subjects

1 Label the pictures.

1 *art*   2 _____   3 _____   4 _____   5 _____

6 _____   7 _____   8 _____   9 _____   10 _____

2 Complete the sentences about you.

1 My favourite subject is _____ .
2 I like _____ too.
3 I don't like _____ and I don't like _____ .
4 I love _____ .
5 I hate _____ .

my words

Do you know more school words?
Write them here.

_____
_____
_____

1 Today is Thursday. Look at David's school timetable. Answer the questions.

	MON	TUE	WED	THUR	FRI
9.00–10.00	maths	computer studies	science	P.E.	history
10.00–11.00	maths	computer studies	science	P.E.	maths
11.00–11.20	BREAK				
11.20–12.30	English	English	history	French	English
12.30–1.30	art	music	maths	geography	English
1.30–2.10	LUNCH				
2.10–3.10	French	P.E.	French	science	science
After school	football	guitar lesson	swimming	football	guitar lesson

1 What day was it yesterday?   *Wednesday*
2 What were the first two lessons?   _____
3 What was the third lesson?   _____
4 What was the fifth lesson?   _____
5 What was the fourth lesson?   _____
6 What was after school?   _____

2 It is now Friday. Are these sentences true or false?

1 Daniel's second lesson yesterday was science.
   false
2 The third lesson on Tuesday wasn't music.
   _____
3 Art wasn't the fifth lesson on Monday.
   _____
4 P.E. was on Tuesday afternoon.
   _____
5 Maths wasn't David's first lesson on Monday.
   _____
6 Geography was after lunch on Thursday.
   _____
7 Science wasn't in the morning on Wednesday.
   _____

Talking Tips!

3 Find seven Talking Tips in the word square. One Talking Tip is in the square twice. Which one is it?

S	T	U	H	P	M	R	O	O	G	E	F	I
D	O	N	T	W	O	R	R	Y	O	R	K	M
I	D	E	N	R	V	E	E	L	A	L	P	O
M	S	T	O	O	C	K	Y	S	W	I	I	V
I	T	S	S	P	O	O	K	Y	A	C	D	E
C	O	F	K	N	O	E	U	C	Y	V	W	O
O	P	T	H	A	L	A	N	O	W	A	Y	V
O	I	L	Y	E	R	S	C	W	A	Y	L	E
R	T	H	A	T	S	N	O	T	F	A	I	R

4 Circle the time words and phrases.

to be: past simple

5 ☆ Circle the correct words.

1 Felix **weren't** / (**wasn't**) at home.
2 He **was** / **were** at his friend's house.
3 Monica and Gemma **was** / **were** at my house last night.
4 It **were** / **was** a good evening!
5 Gemma's homework **weren't** / **wasn't** very good.
6 Her teachers **wasn't** / **weren't** pleased with her.

6 ☆☆ **These sentences are about today.**
Change them and write about yesterday.

1 I am at home today.
  I was at home yesterday.
2 Today is a bad day for Monica.
  Last Tuesday _____
3 Ben isn't at school today.
  _____ yesterday.
4 History and English are in the morning today.
  _____ last week.
5 The French lesson is interesting today.
  _____ yesterday.
6 Ben and Felix aren't at home today.
  _____ yesterday.

to be: past simple questions

7 ☆ Order the words.

1 | funny | the | Was | TV programme | ?
  Was the TV programme funny?
2 | this morning | Ben and Gemma | Were | at school | ?
  _____
3 | yesterday | Was | good | the science lesson | ?
  _____
4 | Were | Monica's | the | chips | ?
  _____
5 | in bed | Felix | last night | Was | ?
  _____
6 | Was | in | your homework | your bag | ?
  _____

8 ☆☆ **Write questions and short answers.**

1 Their first lesson was English. (✓)
  Was their first lesson English?
  Yes, it was.
2 Gemma was in the art room yesterday afternoon. (✗)
  _____
  No, _____
3 Monica was at the library last Saturday. (✓)
  _____
  _____
4 You were at the cinema last Sunday. (✗)
  _____
  _____
5 The children were in the classroom last night. (✗)
  _____
  _____
6 We were at Gemma's house on Sunday. (✓)
  _____
  _____

1 ☆ Find fourteen verbs in the past tense and write them in the table under *Past*.

R	E	M	E	M	B	E	R	E	D	A	L	W
O	F	T	D	S	T	A	R	T	E	D	I	A
S	H	O	U	T	E	D	G	W	N	R	S	T
I	A	R	W	O	S	R	W	E	R	E	T	C
D	I	S	A	P	P	E	A	R	E	D	E	H
U	P	K	S	P	W	A	L	K	E	D	N	E
T	A	L	K	E	D	S	T	U	D	I	E	D
L	I	K	E	D	H	U	R	R	I	E	D	O

Past	Main verb
remembered	*remember*

2 ☆ Now complete the table with the main verbs.

3 ☆ Underline the past tense in these sentences.

1 My friend and I <u>were</u> on the beach last night.
2 We watched the sea for a short time.
3 Then someone shouted for help.
4 A boy was in the sea.
5 My friend and I hurried to the sea.
6 Then … the boy disappeared!
7 We listened … then the boy shouted again. He was OK.

4 ☆☆ Read this letter from Max and answer the questions.

Dear Tilly
I watched the news about the tsunami on TV. It was terrible. The people hurried from the beach and the waves crashed on the beach. Some houses and some people disappeared.
You were great.
You remembered your geography lessons and you helped lots of people.

Well done Tilly!
Max in Germany

1 Was Max in Thailand?
   No, he wasn't.
2 Is he a friend of Tilly's?
   _____
3 How does he know about Tilly?
   _____
4 What disappeared?
   _____
5 Tilly remembered something – what was it?
   _____

Past simple: affirmative

5 ☆ Complete the story with the past tense of the verb in brackets.

Yesterday it ¹**_was_** (be) Saturday.
In the morning Maria ²_____ (stay) at home. She ³_____ (listen) to her MP3 player and she ⁴_____ (watch) TV.
In the afternoon she ⁵_____ (walk) to the park and she ⁶_____ (talk) to her friend Susan. Then they ⁷_____ (go) to the shops.

Past simple: negative

6 ☆ Make these sentences negative.

1 Alex talked to his teacher after the lesson.
Alex didn't talk to his teacher after the lesson.

2 Cheryl liked the French lesson yesterday.

_____

3 Leo did his homework last night.

_____

4 Sophie visited Italy last summer.

_____

5 John had a good holiday in the USA.

_____

6 My brother and sister watched a film at school.

_____

7 ☆☆ Complete the sentences with the negative form of the verb.

1 we / not like the holiday.
We didn't like the holiday.

2 Felix / not watch the film on TV.

_____

3 Ben / not play games on his computer.

_____

4 Monica / not read the news story.

_____

5 Gemma / not arrive at 9 o'clock.

_____

6 Felix / not stay with Gemma.

_____

Past simple: affirmative and negative

8 ☆ Write what Monica and Gemma did and didn't do yesterday in the biology lesson.

Activity	Monica	Gemma
study dolphins	✓	✓
watch a video on sharks	✓	✗
listen to a tape about monkeys	✗	✓

1 Monica _studied dolphins._
2 Monica _____
3 Monica _____
4 Gemma _____
5 Gemma _____
6 Gemma _____

9 ☆☆ Write sentences about you. Write what you did (or didn't do) last weekend. Use these words.

~~help~~ watch walk study listen talk

1 I _helped my sister with her homework._

2 I _____

_____

3 I _____

_____

4 I _____

_____

5 I _____

_____

6 I _____

_____

1 ☆ **Write questions.**

1 You walked to the bus station.
Did you walk to the bus station?

2 We stopped at the post office yesterday.
_____

3 You studied maths last night.
_____

4 They talked on the phone yesterday evening.
_____

5 He shouted to his friend.
_____

6 She hurried to school.
_____

7 You stayed at home on Sunday.
_____

8 They arrived home late.
_____

2 ☆ **Write questions.**

1 we / study history last year?
Did we study history last year?

2 you / watch TV yesterday?
_____

3 they / listen to music yesterday evening?
_____

4 Jacek / like the science lesson last week?
_____

5 Karolina / go to the cinema last weekend?
_____

6 Sofia / talk to her friend in the USA last Saturday?
_____

7 you / talk to the teacher this morning?
_____

3 ☆☆ **Read the text. Ask Ali questions about the words in bold.**

Ali's holiday journal
Last weekend was great. ¹I **played football on Saturday morning** and ²I **watched a film in the afternoon.** The film was really good. ³I **talked to my friend in the evening.** ⁴I **walked to the beach on Sunday morning** and ⁵I **played beach volleyball with my cousins.** ⁶**We watched TV after lunch** and then ⁷**we listened to music in the evening.** I didn't have any homework so the weekend was brilliant!

1 ***Did you play football on Saturday morning?***
2 _____
3 _____
4 _____
5 _____
6 _____
7 _____

4 **Find the feelings words.**

①
thirsty

②
_____

③
_____

④
_____

⑤
_____

⑥
_____

⑦
_____

⑧
_____

5 Think about the past (yesterday, last month, last year, etc.). Write answers about you.

1 When were you bored?
I was bored in French last Thursday.

2 When were you angry?
_____

3 When were you sad?
_____

4 When were you hungry?
_____

5 When were you scared?
_____

6 Put the stickers in the correct place.

> Sticker

① This is my favourite lesson. We learn about different places in the world and about different people and cultures. What is it? It's geography of course!

> Sticker

② What's my favourite subject? I love playing the guitar and I am learning to play the drums too. Reading music is difficult but I like learning about it. What is it? It's music!

7 Complete the report. Use these words.

good   science   ~~like~~

REPORT FROM OUTER SPACE

Hello Fiz!

Thank you for your report.

Did you ¹*like* Kit's science lesson? Fiz, why did you go to school with Kit? You know everything about Earth ² _____ !

We see you were thirsty in Kit's lesson. Was it a ³_____ drink? Can we make it here on our planet?

Your friends from outer space.

Fiz's Learning Blog

Keep an English diary

Write the date. Write in English what you learnt today.
Examples

12th April
I learnt words for school subjects.
I learnt how to talk about the past.
I learnt about Tilly Smith.
I learnt about feelings.

8d Let's Revise!

Vocabulary

1 Find the months.

1 F_____ 3 A_____ 5 M_____
2 S_____ 4 D_____ 6 O_____

2 School subjects. Fill in the missing letters.

1 G _ _ _ R _ _ H _   4 S _ _ _ N _ E
2 H _ _ T _ _ Y   5 M _ _ _ S
3 E _ _ _ I _ H

___/11

Grammar

3 Put the adverb of frequency in the correct place.

1 Do you go to the cinema? OFTEN
_____

2 I do my homework in the evening. USUALLY
_____

3 There is a film on TV at the weekend. ALWAYS
_____

4 We go shopping on a Sunday. NEVER
_____

5 They go to France on holiday. SOMETIMES
_____

4 Complete the sentences with *was* or *were*.

1 Where _____ you yesterday lunchtime?
2 I _____ at home all day yesterday.
3 My friends _____ n't with me.
4 My mum _____ in the house .
5 Where _____ your brothers? I don't know!
6 They _____ n't in the house.

5 Complete the sentences with the past of the verb in brackets.

1 I _____ (stop) at the beach for a drink.
2 It _____ (start) to rain.
3 I _____ (hurry) to the bus station.
4 I _____ (wait) for three hours.
5 The bus _____ (not come)!

6 Write questions. Use the past simple.

1 you / talk / to your friends?
_____

2 Monica / take / a photo?
_____

3 Tilly / visit / Thailand?
_____

4 they / listen / to her?
_____

5 Gemma / go / to swimming practice?
_____

___/21

Functions

7 What's the weather like?

① 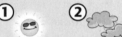 ②   ③   ④

1 It's _____   3 It's _____

2 It's _____   4 It's _____

8 Write the feelings.

①   ②   ③   ④

1 _____   3 _____

2 _____   4 _____

___/8

Your score	Your total score
	___/40

 😃 30–40   🙂 20–30   ☹ 0–20

70

My Picture Dictionary

Entertainment

1 Label the pictures

2 _____

1 *film* _____

The Royal Theatre
Shakespeare's Romeo and Juliet. All summer.

3 _____

ABC CINEMA
Superman – 7.30 p.m.

THE LION KING
Strand Theatre
THE LION KING
23rd May–15th June
A fantastic show with great songs.

BBC1 The Simpsons

6 _____

5 _____

New Art
Pictures by young artists.
The Art Café, 30th June.

4 _____

Pop in the park
The *Arctic Tigers* are at Summer Park.
Saturday 12–4 p.m.

my words

Do you know more entertainment words?
Write them here.

_____
_____
_____

2 What can you see or do? Tick the correct columns.

	concert	exhibition	play	film	musical	TV programme
listen to music	✓		✓	✓	✓	
see dancing						
listen to a story						
see paintings / pictures						
see film stars						

9a Show Time!

Past simple: irregular

1 ☆ Match the verbs and their past forms.

1 go	a was
2 see	b met
3 have	c went
4 meet	d took
5 come	e had
6 is	f came
7 take	g saw

2 ☆ Complete the sentences. Use these verbs in the past tense.

> see   love   meet   have   ~~came~~   go

The musical *Grease* [1] **came** to our town this week.
I [2] _____ yesterday. The show was amazing.
I [3] _____ the music and the songs.
We [4] _____ lots of great dancing.
I [5] _____ some friends after the show.
We [6] _____ a pizza at the theatre café.

3 ☆☆ Make these sentences negative.

1 I went to the theatre last Saturday afternoon.
   I didn't go to the theatre last Saturday afternoon.

2 I bought drinks and an ice cream.
   _____

3 The play was interesting.
   _____

4 The actors were good.
   _____

4 ☆ Look at the table. Complete the sentences.

	Mirari	Ramiro	Klara
go to the cinema	✓	✗	✗
meet some friends	✗	✓	✓
come to my home	✓	✗	✓
see a good film	✓	✓	✗
have an ice cream	✗	✗	✓

1 Mirari **went** to the cinema.
2 Klara didn't _____ to the cinema.
3 Ramiro and Klara _____ some friends.
4 Ramiro _____ to my home.
5 Klara _____ to my home.
6 Mirari and Ramiro _____ an ice cream.

5 ☆☆ Write new sentences about the people in the table.

1 Mirari ***came to my home.***
2 Mirari _____
3 Mirari didn't _____
4 Ramiro and Klara _____
5 Mirari and Klara _____

6 ☆ Complete the text with the past form of the verbs in brackets.

I [1] **went** (go) to an exhibition in our school yesterday. It [2] _____ (be) about toys.
My brother [3] _____ (come) too and we [4] _____ (see) lots of toys from the past.
I [5] _____ (like) the Sindy doll from the 1960s.
She [6] _____ (have) long blonde hair.
My brother [7] _____ (love) the Action Man toys
– they [8] _____ (have) lots of different clothes.
We [9] _____ (take) lots of photos for our school project on Exhibitions.

Reading

7 Read this letter to the Discovery Web Page. Circle the correct words.

> Dear Discovery Web
>
> Last weekend I went with my mum to London. My sister came too. We saw the musical *The Lion King*. It was amazing!
>
> The story was about a young lion in Africa called Simba. His father Mufasa was the king, but his brother Scar, wanted to be king. So Scar didn't like Mufasa and he hated Simba. It was a sad story but it was happy in the end. Simba was the king!
>
> The music was fantastic and all the people in the musical were animals! I liked the music and I loved this musical. It was amazing.
>
> Then we met my cousins and we went for a pizza. I took lots of photos. It was a great day!
>
> Jennifer, Class 5B

THE LION KING
Strand Theatre
THE LION KING
23rd May–15th June
A fantastic show with great songs.

1 Jennifer was in **Africa** / **London** last weekend.
2 She saw a **film** / **musical**.
3 The story was about **lions** / **people**.
4 The king's name was **Scar** / **Mufasa**.
5 Jennifer **liked** / **didn't like** the music.
6 She loved the **film** / **musical**.
7 After the show Jennifer had a **drink** / **pizza**.

8 ☆ Read the text again. Underline all the verbs in the past tense. Write the verbs here.

went _____ _____

_____ _____ _____

_____ _____ _____

9 ☆☆ Which verbs in the text are regular? Which are irregular?

Regular verbs	Irregular verbs
	went

10 ☆☆ Order the words. Write the letters in white and find another musical!

1 saw | a musical | We | in L ondon .
We ***saw a musical in London.***

2 went | w i th | I | my mum .
I _____

3 was | o n | holiday | Sandy .
Sandy _____

4 met | She | a | boy .
She _____

5 The | was | boy's n ame | Danny Zu k o .
The _____

6 wasn't | to Sandy | He | very n i ce .
He _____

7 was | everyo n e | happy | In the end .
In _____

8 fantastic | was | G rease .
Grease _____

The musical is:
The __ __ __ __ __ __ __ __

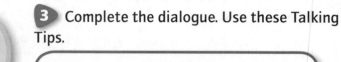

1 Read the dialogue. Answer the questions.

Gemma Hi Ben what are you writing about?

Ben I'm writing about a new film. I saw it last night.

Gemma What did you see?

Ben It was called *Fantastic Four: Rise of the Silver Surfer*.

Gemma Oh yes, Felix went too.

Ben Yes, he did.

Gemma Was it a good film?

Ben I didn't like it very much.

Gemma Did Felix like it?

Ben He loved it. He loves all superhero films.

1 What is Ben doing at the moment?
He's writing about a film.

2 What did he see last night?
_____

3 What did Felix do last night?
_____

4 Did Ben like the film?
_____

5 Did Felix like the film?
_____

6 What films does Felix like?
_____

Talking Tips!

2 Match the phrases to make five Talking Tips.

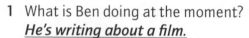

1 No   a you!
2 Come   b it!
3 He's   c way.
4 Poor   d funny!
5 Stop   e on.

3 Complete the dialogue. Use these Talking Tips.

> It's a joke   That's disgusting   ~~move over~~
> How embarrassing   Wait a minute

Gemma Hey, Felix, ¹*move over* . You're sitting in my chair!

Felix Oh, OK.

Gemma It's 4 o'clock. Let's go home.

Monica ²_____ . I want a book from the library first.

Gemma Aagh! There's a frog in my lunch bag. ³_____ ! Felix? Did you do this?

Felix Ha! Ha! ⁴_____ , Gemma!

Monica Oh no! I haven't got any money! Have you got any money, Gemma?

Gemma No, I haven't. Now we can't pay for the ice creams! ⁵_____ .

Past simple irregular: questions

4 ☆ Make these sentences into questions.

1 You saw the TV programme.
Did you see the programme?

2 Ben recorded the wrong programme.
_____

3 Felix watched a different programme.
_____

4 They went to the DVD shop.
_____

5 We saw a basketball match yesterday.
_____

6 He came to the school last week.
_____

5 ⭐⭐ **Read the text. Complete the questions about the underlined parts.**

REVIEW OF *SPIDERMAN* BY ALEX, 11 YEARS OLD.

[1] I saw the film *Spiderman* last night.
The story was about a school student called Peter Parker.

[2] He liked a girl called MJ (Mary Jane). But she liked a different boy.

[3] Peter started to have special powers and then MJ saw him. But he was scared and at first, he didn't talk to her. Then [4] he did lots of things for her.

[5] It was a good film and [6] I liked the actors. I loved Willem Dafoe. [7] He was the Green Goblin in the film. Kirsten Dunst was good too. Spiderman had an amazing red costume and he did a lot of flying – this was great.

1 What *did* Alex *see*?
2 Who _____ Peter Parker _____ ?
3 What _____ Peter _____ to have?
4 _____ he _____ lots of things for her?
5 _____ it a good film?
6 _____ Alex _____ the actors?
7 Who _____ Willem Dafoe in the film?

6 ⭐⭐ **Make these sentences into questions. Write the answer.**

1 you see / programme last night ✓
   Did you see the programme last night?
   Yes, I did.
2 you watch / the new film yesterday? ✗
   _____
3 they go / to the card shop last night? ✓
   _____
4 you wait / at the bus stop this morning? ✓
   _____
5 Dad buy / tickets for a musical? ✓
   _____
6 your brother / play in the volleyball team? ✗
   _____

7 ⭐⭐ **Answer the questions about you.**

1 Did you see a TV programme last night?
   Yes, I did. OR ***No, I didn't.***
2 What did you see on TV last night?
   _____
3 Where did you go last weekend?
   _____
4 Who did you see at school yesterday?
   _____
5 Did you meet your friend last night?
   _____
6 Did you go to the shops yesterday?
   _____

Opinion adjectives

8 **Match the word halves.**

1 fUN   a tastic
2 exc   b ible
3 inter   c iting
4 teRR   d ny
5 fAn   e ing
6 scar   f esTing
7 bOR   g y

1 Find four words and three names from the Earth Explorer story.

L	E	Z	H	I	W	S	K	O
S	P	A	C	E	S	H	I	P
U	E	P	E	L	R	O	T	L
A	J	P	I	Q	P	F	L	A
G	L	E	M	A	L	I	E	N
T	Y	R	F	S	E	Z	U	E
Y	A	E	B	A	N	D	I	T

2 ☆ Complete the story. Use these words.

Then ~~First~~ Finally After that

I listened to a story on the radio. ¹ **First** some aliens came to Earth from a different planet. ² _____ people from Earth saw them and they were scared. ³ _____ the aliens started to laugh! They were funny aliens! But the Earth people didn't laugh. ⁴ _____ the aliens went home. Earth wasn't a funny place!

5 Complete the poem. Find words that rhyme.

cool do ~~end~~ go house new scary stay

You didn't see me, Kit, my friend,
But I watched your planet and in the ¹ **end**
I came to Earth one summer day
And asked you, Kit, 'Can I ² _____ ?'

You took me to a castle and a football match, too
I saw all the things that Earth people ³ _____ ,
I liked all your teachers at your school
Your friends are great and your mum is ⁴ _____ !

Ordering events

3 ☆☆ Write the past tense of the verbs in brackets.

a Then he ¹ **went** (go) to a very cold place and he ² _____ (meet) his mum and dad. He learned he ³ _____ (have) special powers.

b After that he ⁴ _____ (start) work and he ⁵ _____ (meet) a special girl called Lois.

c Finally he ⁶ _____ (help) lots of people on Earth.

d First he ⁷ _____ (stay) with us and he ⁸ _____ (go) to school.

e One day an alien ⁹ _____ (come) to our house. He ¹⁰ _____ (arrive) in a spaceship.

4 ☆☆ The story is mixed up! Order the events in the story.

1 _e_ 2 _____ 3 _____ 4 _____
5 _____

Who was he? _____

But your cat is funny and very hairy
I think Bandit is a little bit ⁵ _____ !
He saw me and thought I was a mouse
He followed me all over the ⁶ _____ !

Earth is good, Earth is blue
It's good I'm visiting somewhere ⁷ _____
But I can't stay – no, no, no!
Home is waiting, so let's ⁸ _____ !

6 Find the correct sticker.

> Sticker

① I've got a big head, two arms, two legs and a long tail. My mouth is really big and I've got lots of teeth. My name is Alien.

> Sticker

② I'm a good alien. I've got lots of friends. We're very good looking aliens. We are all green and have three eyes and big ears.

7 Complete the report. Use these words.

> Where   go   What   Did   come
> dangerous   ~~were~~   zapped

REPORT FROM OUTER SPACE

Dear Fiz

Thank you for your report.

You say there [1]**_were_** aliens at Kit's house and you [2]_____ them. [3]_____ did they do? [4]_____ they disappear? Did they [5]_____ home to their planet? [6]_____ were they from? Are these aliens [7]_____ ?

Fiz, maybe you can [8]_____ home soon.

Your friends from outer space.

Fiz's Learning Blog

Learn verbs

come go have	came went had

come go have

1 Write the verbs in two columns.

2 Fold the paper along the line.

3 Test yourself!

4 Test your friends!

come? came!

go? went!

meet? met!

see? saw!

Learn other words the same way!

Reading

1 Read Monica's blog about Elijah Wood. Answer true or false. Correct the false sentences.

Elijah Wood is a big Hollywood star. He is in *The Lord of the Rings*. He played Frodo Baggins in these three films.

Elijah is American. He has got a brother and a sister. His sister is an actor too.

He went to a school called Avant Studios in his home town. He was a very good actor when he was young, so his mum took him to Los Angeles and he worked on TV.

His first film was *Back to the Future II*, in 1989 and he was only 8 years old. His first big part in a film was in *Avalon* in 1990.

Elijah loves music. He plays the piano and he studied to be a singer too.

1 There were two films called *The Lord of the Rings*.
   false There were three films.

2 He is an English actor.
   _____

3 Elijah Wood started in films when he was young.
   _____

4 *Avalon* was his first film.
   _____

5 He was on TV before films.
   _____

6 Elijah can sing.
   _____

2 Interview Elijah Wood. Write the questions. Use these words:

~~What~~   Who   Have you got   Where

1 ***What is the film called?***
   It's called *The Lord of the Rings*.

2 _____ ?
   I played Frodo Baggins.

3 _____ ?
   I'm from Iowa in the USA.

4 _____ ?
   Yes, I've got a brother and a sister.

3 Irina saw a film on TV last night. Read her report and answer the questions.

I saw a very good film on TV last night. The name of the film was *Galaxy Quest*. In the film, *Galaxy Quest* was a TV programme – there was a spaceship and it went to a different planet every week. The people on the spaceship always helped different aliens.

One day some real aliens came to Earth and asked the actors of *Galaxy Quest* to help them with a problem. The actors went to their planet but in the end they said to the aliens. 'We are not real. We are only actors.' But in the end everyone was happy. It was really funny!

1 What did Irina see last night?
   She saw a good film on TV.

2 What was the name of the film?
   _____

3 Where did the spaceship go every week?
   _____

4 What did the aliens ask?
   _____

5 Where did the actors go?
   _____

6 What did they say to the aliens in the end?
   _____

10 Adventure

My Picture Dictionary

Places and activities

1 Label the pictures.

1 m__ountai__n

2 f _____ t

3 l _____ e

4 c _____ g

5 h _____ g

6 r _____ r

7 m _____
b _____ g

8 r _____
c _____ g

9 c _____ g

2 Find nine adventure words.

A	G	I	N	L	A	K	E	H	O	I	L	M	G
C	A	N	O	E	I	N	G	C	A	H	M	O	P
A	R	G	W	F	O	S	T	I	R	I	N	U	L
M	O	U	N	T	A	I	N	B	I	K	I	N	G
P	K	R	U	A	K	E	M	A	V	I	O	T	E
I	N	F	O	R	E	S	T	F	E	N	J	A	D
N	G	E	P	T	R	T	M	A	R	G	O	I	N
G	E	R	O	C	K	C	L	I	M	B	I	N	G

my words

Do you know more adventure words? Write them here.

_____

_____

_____

_____

_____

_____

10ᵃ Young Explorers

Revision of tenses

1 ⭐ Complete the table.

Verb	Present continuous	Present simple	Past simple
stay	I am ¹ _staying_	I ⁹ _stay_	I ¹⁷ _stayed_
go	I ² _____	I ¹⁰ _____	I ¹⁸ _____
have	he ³ _____	he ¹¹ _____	he ¹⁹ _____
climb	She ⁴ _____	she ¹² _____	She ²⁰ _____
listen	We ⁵ _____	We ¹³ _____	We ²¹ _____
sail	They ⁶ _____	They ¹⁴ _____	They ²² _____
cycle	We ⁷ _____	We ¹⁵ _____	We ²³ _____
rain	It ⁸ _____	It ¹⁶ _____	It ²⁴ _____

2 ⭐ Make these sentences negative.

1 Kate's family is staying at home.
Kate's family isn't staying at home.
2 My dad likes cycling.
_____
3 Granny went climbing.
_____
4 I'm looking for a new adventure.
_____

3 ⭐⭐ Make negative sentences. Use the words below and the correct tense.

1 it / not rain at the moment
It isn't raining at the moment.
2 Sam / not walk in the forest yesterday
_____
3 Lucy and Dave / not like climbing mountains
_____
4 Harry and Max / not go sailing last weekend
_____
5 Stacey / not stay at her friend's house at the moment
_____

4 ⭐⭐ Write a sentence about something you:

1 did last summer
I went on holiday last summer.
2 did last week
_____
3 didn't do yesterday
_____
4 always do on Mondays
_____
5 don't usually do on Sundays
_____

5 ⭐ Complete Katie's letter. Use these words.

> 'm̶   didn't see   play   'm writing
> read   visited   'm sitting   went
> are staying   go   talk

Dear Chloe

I ¹'m on holiday by the sea with my family. We ² _____ in a small house near the beach. At the moment I ³ _____ on the beach and I ⁴ _____ this card to you.

I ⁵ _____ swimming every day and I ⁶ _____ tennis with friends. We haven't got a TV in the house so we ⁷ _____ and ⁸ _____ in the evenings.

Yesterday we ⁹ _____ a big castle. I ¹⁰ _____ any ghosts! After lunch we ¹¹ _____ windsurfing. Fantastic!

See you next week.

Katie

6 ⭐⭐ Complete Chloe's letter. Use the correct form of the verb in brackets.

Dear Katie

I ¹*'m* (be) on an activity holiday in Wales with my brother, James. We ² _____ (stay) in the mountains. At the moment I ³ _____ (wait) for breakfast, so I can write this card to you. The weather ⁴ _____ (be) great – it's hot and sunny.

There ⁵ _____ (be) lots of things to do here. We ⁶ _____ (go) canoeing every morning. In the afternoon we usually ⁷ _____ (go) mountain biking but yesterday we ⁸ _____ (go) rock climbing. It ⁹ _____ (be) fantastic! I ¹⁰ _____ (love) it.

See you next week!

Chloe

7 ⭐⭐⭐ Answer these questions about your holidays.

1 Where did you go last summer?
_____

2 Do you go to this place every summer?
_____

3 Did you go swimming?
_____

4 What was your favourite activity?
_____

5 Who usually goes with you on holiday?
_____

6 Where is your favourite place for a holiday?
_____

7 Why do you like this place?
_____

Reading

8 Read this letter to Discovery Web. Answer the questions.

Hi! My name is Andrew. I'm eleven years old and I'm on a safari holiday in South Africa at the moment with my family.

We went on safari for three days and we saw lots of animals. My favourites were the giraffes and elephants. They're so big!

Today I'm sitting next to the swimming pool. I'm reading a book about animals! There are lots of activities for kids here. In the mornings we can go looking for small animals and in the afternoon we can do painting and sports. I play football in the afternoon. In the evening we sit with the family and talk about the day. This is a really amazing holiday!

1 Where is Andrew on holiday?
He is in South Africa.

2 What did Andrew see on safari?
_____

3 Where is he today?
_____

4 What is he doing?
_____

5 What can children do in the mornings?
_____

6 What does Andrew do in the afternoon?
_____

7 What does Andrew's family do in the evening?
_____

1 Complete the dialogue. Use these questions.

> Do you like canoeing?
> What are you doing at the moment?
> Did Felix come with you?
> ~~What did you do today?~~
> Did you go hiking?

Monica	What a day! I'm really tired!
Ben	¹ _What did you do today_ ?
Monica	I went rock climbing.
Ben	² _____ ?
Monica	No, he didn't come today.
	³ _____ ?
Ben	No! I hate hiking.
Monica	Oh, of course. ⁴ _____ ?
Ben	Yes! Canoeing is my favourite activity!
Monica	OK. Come canoeing with me this afternoon. ⁵ _____ ?
Ben	I'm not doing anything.
Monica	How about having some lunch?
Ben	Good idea. Let's go!

Camping

2 Find the camping words.

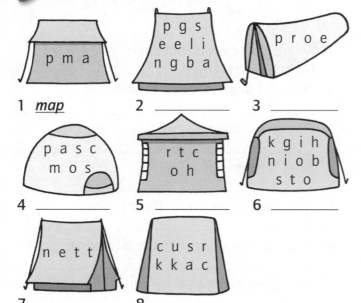

1 _map_ 2 _____ 3 _____

4 _____ 5 _____ 6 _____

7 _____ 8 _____

Talking Tips!

3 Find the Talking Tips.

1 **!looC** _Cool!_

2 **!uoyrooP** _____

3 **!yawaoG** _____

4 **!gnikojer˙uoY** _____

5 **!eramthginas'tI** _____

6 **!gnitsugsids'thaT** _____

7 **!revoevoM** _____

8 **!yrrowtnoD** _____

Revision of tenses

4 ☆ Complete. Use these words.

> Did   Do   Does   Is   Are

1 _Do_ you like hiking?

2 _____ Ben buy a map yesterday?

3 _____ Felix and Gemma canoeing at the moment?

4 _____ Monica writing a Summer Camp webpage today?

5 _____ Monica find her rucksack?

6 _____ Ben and Felix like hiking?

5 ⭐⭐ **Order the words.**

1 [now] [Ben and Felix] [Are]
[playing football] ?
Are Ben and Felix playing football now?

2 [Does] [Ben] [every weekend]
[go climbing] ?
_____

3 [Felix] [go hiking] [Did] [last summer] ?
_____

4 [camping] [Do] [Felix and Gemma]
[like] ?
_____

5 [Ben] [Is] [cooking] [today] [dinner] ?
_____

6 [buy food] [Did] [this morning] [Felix] ?
_____

6 ⭐⭐ **Make questions. Use *Do, Does, Did, Are, Is*. Use the correct tense.**

1 Monica / talk to Ben at the moment?
Is Monica talking to Ben at the moment?

2 Gemma / look for her rucksack at the moment?
_____

3 Ben and Felix / always go hiking at
Summer Camp?
_____

4 Ben / like hiking?
_____

5 you / like mountain biking?
_____

6 you / go camping last summer?
_____

7 Ben and Felix / look for a torch?
_____

7 ⭐ **Read the text. Circle the correct words.**

Fred and Fenella ¹ **go** / (**went**) camping last summer. Fred ² **is loving** / **loved** it but Fenella ³ **hated** / **is hating** it. Fred ⁴ **is going** / **went** canoeing in the river and he ⁵ **was** / **is** very good at it. He is happy in a boat – he ⁶ **sails** / **is sailing** every weekend with his brother. But Fenella never ⁷ **sails** / **sailed**. Poor Fenella – she didn't stay in the canoe!

And ... she can't cook! She ⁸ **phones** / **phoned** a restaurant and ⁹ **is asking** / **asked** them for a pizza! Poor Fred!

8 ⭐⭐ **Make the questions in the correct tense about you. Write the answers.**

1 you / listen to your teacher now?
Are you listening to your teacher now?

2 you eat / cereal for breakfast this morning?
_____

3 What / you do last summer?
_____

4 What / you like doing at the weekend?
_____

5 you / go camping in the summer?
_____

Earth Explorer

1 Read about E.T. Are the sentences true or false? Correct the false sentences.

E.T.

E.T. (Extra Terrestrial) is a famous film by Steven Spielberg. Here is the story:

A family of aliens came to Earth, but when it was time to go, their child (E.T.) didn't go with them. A boy, Elliot, saw E.T. and took him into his house. First it was OK and E.T. and Elliot were good friends. Then E.T. started to feel sad. 'I want to go home, Elliott,' he said. They talked to E.T.'s family and E.T. was ready to go home. But then some bad people took E.T. The film had a happy ending – E.T.'s parents came to Earth again in a spaceship and E.T. and Elliott met them in the forest. The alien family went back home, but Elliott was very sad to say goodbye to his friend.

1 Steven Spielberg made the film E.T. _true_
2 One alien came to earth. _____
3 Elliott took E.T. to the police. _____
4 Elliott and E.T. were friends. _____
5 E.T. wanted to stay on Earth. _____
6 Elliott helped E.T. to go back home. _____
7 E.T.'s brother came to take him home. _____
8 Elliott was not happy at the end. _____

want to

2 ⭐⭐ Order the words.

1 [home] [Fiz] [go] [wants to] .
Fiz wants to go home.
2 [his planet] [wants to] [Fiz] [see] .
_____
3 [family] [Fiz's] [want to] [see him] .
_____
4 [wants to go] [into] [outer space] [Bandit] .
_____
5 [Bandit] [Kit] [on Earth] [wants to have] .
_____
6 [want to] [friends] [Bandit's] [see him] .
_____

3 ⭐⭐ Make the sentences from Exercise 2 negative.

1 _Fiz doesn't want to go home._
2 _____
3 _____
4 _____
5 _____
6 _____

4 ⭐⭐ Now make the sentences from Exercise 3 into questions.

1 _Does Fiz want to go home?_
2 _____
3 _____
4 _____
5 _____
6 _____

5 Write sentences about Kit, his mum and his dad.

	Kit	Kit's mum	Kit's dad
go to New York	✓	✓	
visit Australia	✓	✓	✓
sail to the USA		✓	✓
ride a horse	✓	✓	
learn to windsurf	✓		✓

1 Kit and his mum _want to go to New York._
2 Kit and his mum _____
3 Kit's dad _____
4 Kit's dad _____
5 Kit and his dad _____
6 Kit's mum and dad _____
7 All the family _____

6 Read the holiday information. Put the stickers in the correct place.

①
    Sticker

Active Family holiday – Croatia

Day 1 Arrive in Korana village
Day 2 Cycling
Day 3 Hiking in mountains
Day 4 Canoeing on Black River
Day 5 Free day
Day 6 Go home

②
    Sticker

Climbing on Mount Everest

Day 1 Arrive in Kathmandu
Day 2 Free day
Day 3–5 Hiking
Day 6–12 Mountain climbing
Day 13 Go home

7 Complete the report. Use these words.

Does ~~home~~ sleeping waiting doesn't

REPORT FROM OUTER SPACE

Dear Fiz

Thank you for your report.

You want to come ¹ *home* . But Kit ² _____ want to come with you.

And the cat? ³ _____ Bandit want to come? He is ⁴ _____ in the spaceship. Is this correct? Do you want Bandit with you?

We are ⁵ _____ for you. Come now! Your friends from outer space.

Fiz's Learning Blog

Do revision

Make a revision timetable.

	Vocabulary	Grammar
Monday	Animal words	Present continuous
Tuesday	Adverbs of frequency	Present simple
	Entertainment words	Past simple

Plan what you want to do each day.

Today I want to revise animal words!
Giraffe, dolphin, bat …
Tomorrow I want to revise present simple.
Every day I go to school …

Vocabulary

1 Complete the sentences. Use entertainment words.

1 There's a good f_____ at the cinema.
2 Let's go to the art e_____ in town.
3 *Grease* is a fantastic m_____ .
4 What's your favourite TV p_____?

2 Find the opinion adjectives.

1 RELEIRTB _____   3 NBIGRO _____
2 SCFNTAAIT _____   4 TECIXNGI _____

3 Find four camping words.

1 PAM _____   3 EPOR _____
2 SSAPMOC _____   4 TNET _____

__/12

Grammar

4 Write the past simple.

1 take _____   4 have _____
2 see _____   5 come _____
3 go _____   6 meet _____

5 Write negative past simple sentences.

1 Jane / not meet her friend yesterday.
_____

2 We / not go swimming last week.
_____

3 They / not watch TV last night.
_____

4 My sister / not have dinner yesterday.
_____

6 Answer the questions about you.

1 Did you watch a film on TV last night?
_____

2 What did you do last weekend?
_____

3 Did your friend go to a DVD shop yesterday?
_____

4 What did your friend do this morning?
_____

7 Which tense? *Past simple*, *present simple* or *present continuous*?

1 Kate is sailing around Australia at the moment.
_____

2 Kate has lessons on the boat every day.
_____

3 Kate went to Mexico last year.
_____

8 Make the sentences from Exercise 7 negative.

1 _____
2 _____
3 _____

9 Write the questions. (2 points per question)

1 John / cycle 30 km yesterday?
_____

2 you stay / in a hotel at the moment?
_____

3 your dad / always travel to work by car?
_____

4 you and your sister / watch TV at the weekend?
_____

__/28

Total __/40

Your score   **Your total score**

__/40

😀 30–40   🙂 20–30   ☹ 0–20

10ᵉ Extra Words

Unit 1

1 Find five beach words.

1 llba cebah 3 kys 5 spolf-pilf
2 senud 4 nads

Unit 2

2 Circle five house words.

lampwardrobecookerarmchairwashingmachine

Unit 3

3 Match the halves of the animal words.

1 ko
2 zeb
3 kanga
4 ele
5 b

a ee
b phant
c ala
d ra
e roo

Unit 4

4 Find five food words.

1 likm _____
2 lamaderma _____
3 ngaore ceiju _____
4 terubt _____
5 tstoa _____

Unit 5

5 Find five things you can find in the living room.

rugplantcandlecushionTVremotecontrol

Unit 6

6 Match the words to make objects in town.

1 shopping
2 post
3 diving
4 zebra
5 traffic

a crossing
b lights
c trolley
d box
e board

Unit 7

7 Find five Hallowe'en words.

Unit 8

8 Write the correct words.

1 You can see lots of countries on this. _____
2 The teacher writes on this. _____
3 You can read and write on these. _____
4 You play music on these, e.g. a guitar. _____
5 You paint with this. _____

Unit 9

9 Find five theatre words.

Unit 10

10 Write the correct words.

1 Put your h _ _ _ _ t on your head
2 Ride in a c _ _ _ e on the river.
3 Go rock climbing up a c _ _ ff.
4 Sleep in a t _ _ t when you camp.
5 Go swimming in a l _ _ e.

Pearson Education Limited
Edinburgh Gate
Harlow
Essex CM20 2JE
England

and Associated Companies throughout the world.

www.pearsonelt.com

© Pearson Education Limited 2010

The right of Kate Wakeman to be identified as the author of this Work
has been asserted by them in accordance with the Copyright, Designs
and Patents Act 1988.

All rights reserved; no part of this publication may be reproduced,
stored in a retrieval system, or transmitted in any form or by any
means, electronic, mechanical, photocopying, recording, or otherwise
without the prior written permission of the Publishers.

First published 2009
Ninth impression 2017
Twelfth impression 2018

ISBN 978-1-4082-0935-6

Set in 12/15pt ATQuay Sans Book and 12/15pt ATQuay Medium

Printed in Malaysia (CTP-VVP)

Authors' acknowledgements

Illustrated by Andrew Hamilton, Andy Peters, Julian Mosedale,
Piers Baker, Rob Davis and Sean Longcroft.

Photo Acknowledgements

The publisher would like to thank the following for their kind
permission to reproduce their photographs:

(Key: b-bottom; c-centre; l-left; r-right; t-top)

pages 2 Martin Beddall: (l, c, r); 4 Martin Beddall; 5 Getty Images:
Laurence Griffiths; 7 Ronald Grant Archive: Walt Disney / Pixar (tl);
Walt Disney (br). Kobal Collection Ltd: Hannah Barbera Prods / Atlas
Entertainment (tc). Moviestore Collection Ltd: (bc); Disney (tr). Rex
Features: c. W. Disney / Everett (bl); 8 Martin Beddall; 10 PunchStock:
Comstock Images; 11 Getty Images: Photodisc; 13 Jupiter Unlimited:
liquidlibrary; 14 Alamy Images: Photos 12 (r). Aquarius Collection:
Disney / Pixar (l). Kobal Collection Ltd: The Kobal Collection /
Aardman Animations / Dreamworks (cr). Rex Features: Everett
Collection (cl); 16 Martin Beddall: (l, r); 17 Martin Beddall; 19 Rex
Features: South West News Service; 20 iStockphoto: Jo Ann Snover;
23 www.dreamstime.com: Graham Tomlin (monkey); Javarman (bat);
Jjmaree (turtle). iStockphoto: Holger Wulschlaeger (shark); Ivan van
Rensburg (giraffe); Jessica Bethke (chameleon); Karen Givens (tiger);
Kristian Sekulic (dolphin); Omar Ariff (elephant); Roberto A Sanchez
(parrot). PunchStock: image100 / Wildlife Wonders (squirrel); 25
www.dreamstime.com: Dcshea (tr). iStockphoto: Christopher Russell
(bl); 26 Thumbs Up (UK) Ltd; 27 Martin Beddall: (t, b); 30 FLPA
Images of Nature: Minden Pictures / Fred Bavendam (tl). iStockphoto:
Baldur Tryggvason (bl). Seapics.com: Tom Haight (tr);
33 Martin Beddall: (l, c, r); 40 Getty Images: AFP; 41 Getty Images:
Stone / Photo and Co; 42 iStockphoto: Zlatko Kostic; 46 www.
dreamstime.com: Pixlmaker (f); Yiannos1 (e). iStockphoto: (a);
Andreas Gradin (b); Elena Elisseeva (c); Glenda Powers (d); 50 Martin
Beddall; 55 Alamy Images: foodfolio (tl); Johnny Greig (bl). Art
Directors and TRIP photo Library: Helene Rogers (tr). DK Images:
Dave King (br); 56 Martin Beddall: (t, b); 59 Corbis: Reed Kaestner;
62 iStockphoto: Jose Manuel Gelpi Diaz; 71 Alamy Images: Content
Mine International (br). Ronald Grant Archive: Walt Disney (c).
Kobal Collection Ltd: Warner Bros / DC Comics (l). Rex Features:
Dan Tuffs (tr); 73 Ronald Grant Archive: Walt Disney; 74 Martin
Beddall: (t, b); 76 Kobal Collection Ltd: Warner Bros / DC Comics; 78
Martin Beddall; 79 Alamy Images: Robert Estall Photo Agency (bl).
iStockphoto: Alexey Fursov (tl); Ben Blankenburg (tr, bc); Eric Foltz
(br); 81 Corbis: Randy Faris

All other images © Pearson Education

Picture Research by: Sarah Purtill

Every effort has been made to trace the copyright holders and we
apologise in advance for any unintentional omissions. We would
be pleased to insert the appropriate acknowledgement in any
subsequent edition of this publication.